# PAST AND POSITIVE

# SELECT PUBLICATIONS
## (PUBLISHERS OF FINE POETRY)

## PRESENTS

# PAST AND POSITIVE

# By

# DENNIS J. PENFOLD

First published in Great Britain 1998

by

SELECT PUBLICATIONS

(Publishers of Fine Poetry)
5 LISTER ROAD
TILBURY
ESSEX
RM18 8YH

Printed by:
ProPrint
Riverside Cottage
Great North Road
Stibbington
Peterborough PE8 6LR

ISBN: 0 9530630 3 8

Cover Design
by
ANTHONY THOMAS

# CONTENTS:

PAGE NO:

The sun was always shining,
my heart was full of joy,
those happy days that I loved so,
when I was just a boy.

The world somehow seemed different,
the pace of life was slow,
my eyes begin to fill with tears,
as memories fondly flow.

I look back with nostalgia,
it's just like a sweet refrain,
I would change but not a single day,
if I could live my life again.

# FOREWORD

Dennis Penfold's poems not only contain a treasure chest of memories, they are of a unique quality, and steeped in history!
Every one of Dennis's poems make compelling reading.
They are of superb interest from cover to cover, and their popularity leaves nothing to be desired.
They make you laugh they make you cry and they seem to roll off the tongue like magic!
After reading Dennis Penfold's poems, they leave you longing for more!

Editor

SELECT PUBLICATIONS (P.O.F.P.)

# PAST AND POSITIVE

It was Christmas week up the Old High Street.
My wife sent me up for some chops.
The bottom end of it was empty,
As I gazed at the boarded up shops.

I wandered along to the butchers,
My heart felt as heavy as lead.
Through the window I looked at the prices,
And I came out with mincemeat, instead!

It made me feel rather despondent,
As further along my feet plod,
I was almost down to my last shilling,
Till my pension was due, 'Oh thank God.'

I glanced at each stall in my passing,
At necklaces, brooches and rings,
Slippers, underwear, clothing,
They all seemed to sell the same things!

I thought to myself, 'Oh how boring?'
It wasn't like this years ago!
Nearly every stall had something different,
down the market of Old Walthamstow.

I got fed up with looking at sportswear,
Pot-pourri, cosmetics, cheap scent,
In the walk-around shops on their counters,
'Twas the same thing wherever I went!

Not a smile, did I see on folk's faces
Where was this spirit of 'Good cheer?'
I was transported back to my childhood,
To these days which I cherished, most dear.

I'm afraid that I did not feel festive
In this season of 'Good-will and Joy'
As I sat on the seat outside Woolworth's,
Thinking back to when I was a boy.

The market was better in those days,
When I used to go up there with mum,
I always looked forward to going
And pleaded with her, 'Let me come!'

The shops were still open till midnight,
The stalls, they stayed out until ten,
The goods were sold at knockdown prices,
That's what our sweet life, was like then.

In my mind, I could see it all clearly,
The High Street, how it used to be,
Crowded with happy faced shoppers,
As they bustled along in their glee.

They were bidding for all types of bargains,
At prices that they could afford
If you had a few bob in your pocket,
Then you could live just like a Lord.

On the corner, the Salvation Army
Were gathered together in song,
With their 'tambourines, cornets and trumpets,'
Neath the lamp-light, that down on them shone.

The atmosphere then, was delightful,
The people, were thoughtful and kind.
They were not so greedy in those days,
What a pity, we've left them behind.

I have come to the end of my story,
When  the naphtha flares hissed on the stalls,
When the High Street was bathed in its glory,
As my nostalgic mind still recalls.

I wandered back home full of memories,
Of all the good times that have passed,
I'm afraid we all took them for granted,
But alas, they were too good to last!

# THE CURSE OF POVERTY

It's the same the world over,
if you're poor, then poor, you'll stay,
money always goes to money,
it has always been that way.
It's an unfair world we live in,
as we struggle on in vain,
for some, life is all sunshine,
for others, it's all rain.

When young, I saved my pennies,
'What a shame we were so poor,'
To buy my mum a cottage,
with roses round the door.
Alas, my dreams were shattered,
good intentions though they were,
my sacrifice was not enough,
though I did it all for her.

With the cards that God has dealt us,
we play our hand to win,
being poor is our misfortune,
Isn't poverty a sin?!
Life is full of 'Have, and Have nots,'
wishful dreams are all in vain,
I would give all my possessions,
just to have mum back again!

# HAIL MOSLEY

I remember so clearly when I was a lad.
The most devastating shock of my life, which I had!
I'd gone shopping up the High Street, with my dear old mum.
I almost begged her to 'Please, let me come!'
I loved the old High Street, it was like a day out,
it was different in those days, without any doubt.

'Lidstones the Draper's,' was her first port of call.
Before she continued to pause at each stall.
She stopped at the Fish stall for some haddock for dad's tea,
and 'two pen'orth of herrings, for herself, and for me!

We went to St. James Street, mum had more stuff to buy,
over the road, a crowd gathered, and I wondered why! ---
When she'd finished her shopping, mum said, 'I'll be blowed,'
'I wonder what's going on over the road?' ---

What possessed mum to do it, I really can't say,
but the shock which it gave me, still lives on to this day!
It was in Leuchar Road, where the meeting took place,
we stood at the corner, where there was much more space.
A vast crowd had gathered, it was packed like Sardines,
determined to stay there, mum did, by all means!

I began to get frightened, and said 'Let's come away!'
But mum would not listen, and decided to stay!
It was shortly after, when 'Up pulled a Van!'
And 'Out, tumbled Mosley, with the rest of his Clan.
As the situation worsened, things looked very bleak!
The spectators around him, would not let him speak!
fighting broke out in the middle of the road,
mounted police drew their truncheons, and blood, freely, flowed!

Being young as I was, I was shaking with fright,
never in my life, had I see such a fight.
Mum looked for an exit, to make good our escape,
in the turmoil that followed, with the way things took shape.
To this very day, I remember it well,

those terrified people, who 'stumbled, and fell!'
Too late, mum regretted, being caught in the din,
as wielding their truncheons, the police waded in!

'Never again would I do this,' mum vowed,
and spotting an opening, we slipped through the crowd.
Making good our escape, made me feel so relieved,
for that 'Horrific Scene,' you would not have believed!
It taught mum a lesson, she would never forget,
for her foolish decision, she lived to regret.

With the shock that it gave me, I was still feeling bad,
when mum told dad what had happened, 'He nearly went mad!'
He made my mum promise, that 'never again,'
to repeat what she'd done, which he termed, 'So insane!'
I can still see it now, since those years long ago,
'Oswold Mosley, 'The Black-shirts,' 'Leuchar Road,' 'Walthamstow.'

## A NICE BIT 'O CLOTH

The coat that dad bought me, came down to my feet,
and I loathed to be seen in it out in the street.
When the other kids saw me, I felt such a twit,
dad said 'as you grow taller, the better, the fit.'
Dad bought it one Sunday for me up the Lane,
and I had to wear it coming home on the train.
The carriage was crowded, and several eyes stared,
Some sniggered, some giggled, my feelings weren't spared.
When I complained, my ole dad showed his wrath,
saying 'What you've got there, is a nice bit 'O cloth.'
By the time Dad had finished, I was almost in tears,
as for all of my pleading, only fell on deaf ears.

'You've got a good bargain,' said the man on the stall,
as dad glanced at the others, which were hung on the wall.
But it looks much too long,' I cried to my dad,
and the more that I pleaded, the more he got mad.
It cost my ole dad all of seven and a tanner,

and he said I looked just like the Lord of the manor.
'That's your problem solved,' said my dad with a smile,
I felt down in the dumps, for I thought it looked vile.
Though young that I was, I still had my pride,
and I couldn't explain just how I felt inside.
Twas no shame in the thirties, to be short of money,
wearing secondhand clothes, well it wasn't too funny.
Though under the circumstances, dad did his best,
for it wasn't too easy, to keep us well dressed.

On Monday morning when I went to school,
the kids, they all laughed, and I felt such a fool.
I felt my face flush, and I thought, damn, and blast,
as my red ears detected, the remarks that were past.
How could my ole dad subject me to this,
and I thought if I lost it, it would not come amiss.
Kids could be cruel with the things that they say,
and I was in torment, for the rest of the day.
'You look like an Undertaker,' a nasty kid spat,
'All you need now, is a shiny, top hat.' ---

To me, it was like a red rag to a bull,
when the kids took the mickey out of me at the school.
After all said and done, it wasn't my fault,
if that was the coat that my father had bought
We were brought up in those days to do as was told,
the only good thing about it, It kept out the cold,
Oh if only the bloody thing wasn't so long,
and oh boy, did I hate it, when I had it on.
My school work, it suffered, and I knew just why,
I was being tormented, and wished I could die.
All over that overcoat, my life, it was hell,
never was I so glad, to hear the school bell.
I would shoot from the classroom as quick as I could,
oh if I had the courage to lose it, 'I would.'

All through the winter, I wore it each day,
for that's all that I had to keep warm, come what may.

When the other kids shivered, I felt nice, and snug,
in fact, I felt just like a bug in a rug.
I was glad of it when the snow started to fall,
perhaps my ole dad, he was right after all?


## LIVINGSTONE ROAD

Back in the twenties our humble abode,
was a two bedroom flat down in Livingstone Road.
We were destined to live in that flat for eight years,
where my frustrated mother was often in tears.
It was shared with the Pavey's, our neighbour below,
who were blessed with three children, that our dear Lord bestow.

It wasn't a place one could look on with pride,
with its two up, two down, and a toilet outside.
Our room was so small, there was no space to play,
we were everlasting getting, in each other's way.
There was five of us kids, without mum and dad,
and our crowded conditions, drove my poor mother mad.
'For Gawdsake get out from my feet,' she would say,
'Go out the street where there's more room to play.'
Sometimes in frustration, she'd give us a clout,
round the back of our head, as we rushed to get out.

Many a time my poor mum was upset,
her decision to come there, she lived to regret,
The kitchen we lived in, was depressingly small,
with its little stone sink, sticking out from the wall.
A 'Dresser,' a 'Cupboard,' which was far from ideal,
and a 'Blackleaded Range,' where she cooked us a meal.
The window looked down on the garden below,
where a handful of flowers used to struggle to grow.
It was shared with the Pavey's, who were out there each night,
we had the left side, and they had the right.
My father kept chickens, - he built a small run,
at the back of the garden, in the shade from the sun.
It wasn't too bad, till the buggers got out,

and Suddenly, one of the neighbours would shout,
'I've got your cock over here, Mr Pen,'
Who had to retrieve it? - 'Why poor bloody, Den.' ---

Leading off from the scullery downstairs, was the yard,
and keeping it tidy, I must say was hard.
All the old junk, used to congregate there,
including the dustbin, and an old broken chair.
A bucket, and scrubbing brush, stood by the drain,
which constantly overflowed from the rain.
The lav in the garden, had a tongue and groove door,
a well scrubbed deal seat, and a concreted floor,
Its cobwebby walls, showed signs of decay,
where the paint, and the plaster, had fallen away.
Small squares of paper, was part of the scene,
it was taken in turns, to keep the place clean.
Twas a paradise for spiders, that crawled from the eaves,
I was scared they would crawl up my trousers, and sleeves.
Many a cold night, Win waited outside,
whilst I tended my needs, and sat there dreamy eyed.
'Fer Gawdsake, 'urry up, I'm frozen,' she'd cry, ---
till at last I came out, with the candle held high.
'What took yer's 'long?" - snapped  my Win in her plight,
'I thought you were going ter be in there all night.' ---

The old iron bath that mum used I recall,
hung up by a nail in the yard on the wall.
On bath night, we undressed in front of the hearth,
whilst downstairs mum  went, to drag up the old bath.
It was an Ordeal, for my overworked mum,
though she tried to keep cheerful, she always looked glum.
Once every week, my poor mum had to toil,
with filling up saucepans of water to boil.
To bath us, she had to kneel down on the floor,
no one today, would have envied her chore.
'Bad enough, you may think, but That wasn't all, ---
emptying the bath, --- 'That was the gall.' ---
When this was done, it was time for our bed,

as mum bade us goodnight, with a kiss on the head.
'I slept in the same room as my mum and dad,
as being the youngest, and still a wee lad.
Mum thumped the flock mattress to smooth out the lumps,
though her hard work and effort, still resulted in bumps.
Next to the door, stood my mum's chest of drawers,
who's bottom was scratched, by our pussycat's claws.
A few broken ornaments, stood on the top,
with the paraffin lamp, supervised by my pop.
Next to that, stood a half bottle of Sloans,
for mum's rheumatic joints, and her arthritic bones.

In the bay window, stood the Artpot and Ped,
with its large matching Poe, which sat under the bed.
We were glad it was there, when it came to our aid,
it was put to good use, and it did a good trade.
The first thing dad did, was to wind the two clocks,
whilst he sat on the bed, in his longjohns, and socks.
He pulled out his teeth, which he dropped in a glass,
then instructed my mum, to shift over her arse.
He snuggled up close to my mum in the bed,
'For Christsake stop fidgeting Nell,' - my dad said.
During the night, I could hear my dad snore,
it would keep me awake, and became quite a bore.
I would feel so relieved when the morning came round,
and he'd swear to us all he did Not make a sound.---

A line of damp washing, was hung in the room,
on mum's indoor clothes line, to add to our gloom.
Dad's long pants and vest, was draped over a chair,
in front of the fire, to help them to air.
It took a few days for the washing to dry,
and dad dunked his head every time he walked by.
It made him bad tempered, and he showed off with mum,
snatching things down, he was mad as they come.
'You'll 'ave ter put up with it Stan,' mum would cry,
'How else do yer think I can get em to dry?' ---
Hanging up with the washing, was my mother's cane,

it was there to control us, when words were in vain.
We could be little buggers at times, I must say,
though more often than not, we would get our own way.

I loved to watch navvies, repairing our road,
with pickaxe and shovel on shoulder they strode.
Stripped to their shirtsleeves, they hammered away,
standing there watching them work, made my day.
Their fourteen pound hammers struck the head of the spike,
with rhythmic aimed blows, and such accurate strike.
When the task of their labour was almost complete,
along came the steamroller, down our long street.
Backwards and forwards, it chugged to and fro,
when I think of it now, How my sweet memories flow. ----

I remember the Tradesman, that went door to door,
the Milkman, the Baker, and quite a few more.
The Carbolic man on his round would come by,
'Beat the bugs.' 'Beat the bugs,' 'Beat the bugs!' was his cry.
Then round came the Ragman, with sack on his back,
in his cloth cap and muffler, and dirty old mack.
Mum used to rely on this man a great deal,
for he made all the difference, whether we had a meal.

Livingstone Road overflowed with its kids,
'George's, Tommy's, Billy's, and 'Sid's.' ---
They weren't what you'd call, bad little chaps,
though sometimes their squabbles, turned into scraps.
Snotty nosed urchins, with scabs on their knees,
played knocking down ginger, and peed against trees.
With the arse out their trousers, and spuds in their socks,
they teased, and chased girls, putting hands up their frocks.
The women wore caps, as they stood at their gates,
watching the kids on their scooters, and skates.
They could be a rough handful at times, so they can,
they could swear like a trouper, and fight like a man.

I loved Sunday dinners, they were a real treat,
and mum's batter puddings, you just couldn't beat.

Even today, I still relive those scenes,
the steam on the window, the smell of the greens.
The snores of my parents, in their afternoon nap,
with the News Of The world, slipping down from their lap.
Sunday nights, - How I loathed them, early bed, was the rule,
for getting up Monday, and going to School.
Dad would start to get fidgety around half past eight,
and say 'Come on my Cockbird, it's getting quite late.'
When he filled up the lamp, twas then I could see,
that Sunday was well and truly over for me. ---

We had a hard time in those days long ago,
how my parents existed, I'll just never know.
The working class people, they had a rough deal,
and some did not know when they'd see their next meal.
Pathetically, dole queues, grew longer each day,
and the poor unemployed, got a Cut in their pay.
Pawnshops grew busy, with queues at their door,
by the increase in poverty, and the plight of the poor.
Many a time, my poor mum pledged her ring,
or a bundle of clothes, which she tied up with string.
The stigma of poverty, I recall to this day,
and my mum's flowing tears, as she wiped them away. ---

When mum got a letter from the Agent, 'Chas Hare,
she said that the Dear Lord had answered her prayer.
As she read the letter, her face was aglow,
she was offered a house, in her Beloved Walthamstow.
She pleaded to dad, with her tongue in her cheek,
for the asking rent was, 'Twenty five bob per week!.'
Though dad was reluctant at first, strange to say,
in the end my dear mother, she got her own way.
The following Saturday, at nine in the morn,
the Removers came round with a toot on their horn.
Out came mum's furniture, mangle and all,
two journeys were made, because the van was too small.
Goodbyes were exchanged as the van pulled away,
to our new destination, where our future lay.

Twas the happiest day of my dear mother's life,
dad said she deserved it, she was a good wife.
After eight years of misery in Livingstone Road,
at last we were heading to our new abode.
That was back in the thirties, and I'll never forget,
that letter from mum's landlord, of a 'Nice house to let.'
We lived there for years till the Second World War,
and for the last time, we closed its front door.
We moved to Keith Road, which was not far away,
but That's another story, I'll tell you some day.'


## MUM'S LOT

You could say that dad, was a very Shrewd man!
A chip off the block of the old, Penfold Clan.
His philosophy in life, was to try to attain,
a healthy, bank balance, without too much strain..
He was very thrifty, and would try to make do,
with secondhand goods, in preference to new!
Like his father before him, dad always thought twice,
before buying new, if the old, would suffice.

When mum asked for more money, he would not relent,
and she had to account for each shilling, she spent!
Each day was a worry as she struggled to cope,
and as for an increase, she abandoned all hope!
The clothes on her back, they had seen better days,
and the way that she managed, earned everyone's praise.
Day, after day, it was always the same,
not a penny, poor mum, did she have to her name!

Our home, though quite modest, she kept nice and clean,
for it was her palace, and mum, was the Queen.
Though several years wed, her possessions were few,
and the stuff that she had, I must say, was not new!
An upright piano, was mum's Pride and Joy,
which she always kept polished, since I was a boy.

In her bay window, stood her Artpot and Ped,
on mum's faded lino, which was once, turkey red.

Two elegant vases dominated the shelf,
and a Westminster chimer, was the soul of her wealth!
What to do with the sofa! mum hadn't a clue,
there were holes in the seat where its springs had poked through.
She hid them with cushions, they were dark, chocolate brown,
but they found their way through, everytime you sat down!
The chairs weren't too bad, though they suffered from ware,
Dad said, 'They're alright if you used them with care!
But after a time, the seats started to sag,
dad said, 'all that mum did, was to 'nag, nag, nag, nag!'
Although easy going, what gave mum the ike,
was when dad used the room for repairs to his bike!
Had she put her foot down right from the start,
I'm sure not so often, she would have lost heart.
He wasn't a man for his home! my ole dad,
and his untidy ways seemed to drive my mum mad.
Being too placid, my poor mum paid the price,
for refusing to listen to good, sound, advice!
She gave in too easy, 'that was her trouble,'
for 'who else would put up with a roomful of rubble?'

This was the story of my mother's life,
A hardworking woman, good mother, and wife.
She cared for her family, as each day went by,
without sign of a grumble, a tear or a sigh.
Till the end of her life, she had given her all,
and her sweet natured spirit, to this day I recall!
If ever a medal had been earned, Well by gum,'
I am sure the good Lord, he would pin one on mum!

# PAPA WEIRISCH

My Grandad was a dear old soul, who was loved by one and all,
This is the story of his life, which proudly, I recall.
He was born in a place called Merkheim, in eighteen seventy four,
and came to live in England, long before the First World War.
His childhood days were happy, his parents, he adored,
he seemed to wallow in their love, which from their hearts, they
poured.
They used to think the world of him, 'There was no one like their
boy,'
to them, he was an angel, who filled their hearts with joy.

His father had a lovely house, which overlooked the Rhine,
where grapes grew in abundance, from his overhanging vine.
They would sit out in their garden, on a warm, and sunny day,
and watch the steamers passing by, as they went on their way.
He had a childhood sweetheart, Leichner, was her name,
they would meet outside the Village Forge, at the bottom of the lane.
He worshipped the 'ground she walked on,' she was his very life,
he vowed the day when he grew up, that she'd become his wife.
Her silken hair, was soft and fair, her eyes were violet blue,
she was his love, and only love, 'Never was a love so true.' ---
Hand in hand, they used to stand, outside the Blacksmith's door,
where they loved to watch the sparks flow, and to hear the bellows
roar.
The ringing of the anvil, was like music to their ears,
the Smithy got to know them, and would cry, 'Come in my dears.' ---
They watched him shape the horse shoes, before their very eyes,
then he'd plunge them in the water, and a cloud of steam would
rise.
They loved to see the horses shod, it gave them quite a thrill,
they were filled with admiration, for the Smithy, and his skill.

Every day they used to meet, when they came out from school,
they would gather bluebells from the woods, until their arms were
full.
As they skipped along the leafy lane, they were full of happiness,
and his sweetheart looked so pretty, in her little yellow dress.
Her father was a baker, the locals called him Fred,
and each day from the bakehouse, came the smell of new baked
bread.
As they stood outside the little shop, in its window, they would gaze,
Never could there ever have been, such sweeter, childhood days.
They were given apfelstrudel, from her mother's loving hand,
and they savoured every morsel, for it always tasted grand.
Before he left her to come home, they always used to kiss,
enraptured in each other's love, in their world of utter bliss.

Though she was the lovelight of his life, 'alas, they had to part,'
her parents came to England, and 'it broke his poor young heart.' ---
His life became so empty, things could never be the same,
and he became more sadder, with every day that came.
His parents, they did everything, to try and make amends,
and often they went out their way, to introduce new friends.
He seemed to lose the will to live, as he pined for her each day,
he could not eat, he could not sleep, since they stole his love away.

The years rolled by, and he grew up, into a fine young man,
he never divulged to a living soul, the secret of his plan.
When he became eighteen years old, he knew what he must do
he decided to come to England, where he'd start his life a'new.
When the day arrived to 'bid goodbye, 'it broke his parents heart,
they never quite got over it, from the day he did depart.
His father was so bitter, and he never did forgive,
he cast him from his family, for as long as he shall live. ---

He found himself a small back room, somewhere in Kentish Town,
he kept thinking of his mother, and it made him feel so down.
He roamed the streets of London, in his search which was in vain,
he could not find employment, and his sunshine, turned to rain.
A stranger in a foreign land, without a single friend,

15

he wondered when his luck would change, and his misery would
end.
Every night when he came home, in his room, he'd sit and mope,
feeling tired, and hungry, 'He almost gave up hope.'
With his spirit almost broken, he trudged from street to street,
only stopping now'n again, to rest his aching feet.
His clothes became quite shabby, as week by week, rolled by,
he was living like a pauper, and he wished that he could die. ---

As Destiny would have it, when down to his last bob,
he came across a baker's shop, whilst looking for a job.
He gazed into the window as he stood outside the shop,
he felt so weak with hunger, he was almost fit to drop.
To satisfy his hunger, he decided on a roll,
for being without food all day, it began to take its toll.
He clutched a penny in his hand, as he walked through the door,
'Never once in all his life, had he ever been so poor.' ---
He stood before the counter, there was no one to be seen,
he heard voices in the outer room, above the whirl of the machine.
He felt so thoroughly miserable, as he pondered on his strife,
when suddenly before him, 'stood the Sweetheart of his life.'
He thought he must be dreaming, and he pinched himself to see,
for he just could not believe his eyes, 'How could this possibly be?
They fell into each other's arms, his eyes were wet with tears,
fate brought them back together, after all those long, lost years.
She led him through to the back room, and sat him down to eat,
then pulling off his boots, and socks, she bathed his swollen feet.
This act of love, and kindness, made the poor boy really sob,
her parents, they both pitied him, and offered him a job./
Twas the ending of a nightmare, just like a dream come true,
not only had he found a job, but his long lost, sweetheart too.

Eventually they married, and they raised a family,
with three sons, and two daughters, they were happy as could be.
They often talked about old times, they loved to reminisce,
they both relived their childhood days, inbetween each passionate
kiss.
They adored their little children, there was Peter, Fred and Jack, ---

Helena and Sophie, who had long hair down her back.
The two girls were inseparable, like two peas in a pod,
idolised by both, their parents, who worshipped the ground they trod.
They adored the streets of London, the bright lights and the shops,
where in the back streets, they would play, with their wooden hoops,
and tops.
They would go to Berwick Market, roam around the stalls,
and gaze with admiration, at the bright lit, music halls.
Covent Garden was their favourite place, where often, they would
play,
then they'd skip along to Drury Lane, which was almost every day.

Jacob joined the Merchant Navy, at the age of twenty three,
though hard he tried, he could not hide, his passion for the sea.
He'd fulfilled his life's ambition, he travelled far, and wide,
though his absence broke his parents heart, they looked on him with
pride.
He looked handsome in his uniform, with gold braid on his sleeve,
they welcomed him with open arms, when he came home on leave.

Grandad had a baker's shop, in the busy part of town,
he valued all his customers, and never let them down.
I believe it was in Soho, if my memory serves me right,
they did not have much leisure, for they slaved from morn, till night.
This lovely German couple, would give bread to the poor,
and tragedy struck them once again, at the outbreak of the War;
In spite of all their kindness shown, they could not seem to win<
for when the First World War broke out, their windows were
smashed in.
Their piano in the upper room, was flung into the street,
then satisfied with what they'd done, their deed was then complete.

Though people used to scorn them, the couple bore no malice,
Grandad was incarcerated, at Alexandra Palace.
Once again, they both were parted, 'Oh how cruel life can be,'
and to crown it all, they lost two sons, who both died with T.B. ---
Peter died at seventeen, followed shortly by poor Fred,
the family were heartbroken, and many tears were shed.

They refused to let poor Grandad, attend the funeral of his Son,
the authorities forbade it, 'What harm could he have done?' ---
When the War was over, Grandad looked like skin and bone,
Nell and Sophie by then, were married, and had families of their
own.

Grandma Weirisch passed away at the age of fifty four,
they did everything they could for her, till they could do no more.
Poor Grandad's life was shattered, his world was at an end,
not only did he lose his wife, but a very dear, dear, friend.
On the morning of the funeral, when the cortege left the house,
friends, and neighbours, dofft their hats, in respect for his dear
                                                        Spouse.
The sorrow deep within his heart, he knew, would never ease,
he said, 'If they knew a Saint was passing, they would go down on
                                                        their knees.'
What a wonderful compliment for a man to pay unto h is wife,
may her soul find peace in Heaven, and everlasting life. ---

Papa Weirisch, after his wife's death, was a very lonely man,
it was plain to see upon his face, how much he missed my Gran.
He visited his family, regular each week,
and when he talked of Grandma, the tears ran down his cheek.
They had been a closeknit family, where love it knew no bounds,
for they idolised each other, fantastic, though it sounds.
When he came to see them, he never stayed too long,
he was always glad to get back home, to where his heart belong. ---
He lived with all his memories, the happy, and the sad,
and he thanked the Lord for giving him, the good life that he'd had.
He lived to be a ripe old age, before he passed away,
that was the story of his life, There's not much more to say. ---
Interned in Queens Road Cemetery, in dear old Walthamstow,
that's where his body lies in rest, --- The Grandad I loved so.
My mum and dad, and auntie Soph, they also lie in there,
whenever I go, before I leave, I stop to say a prayer
I hope they're re-united, all those people that I love,
to dwell in peace forever more, in God's Heaven up above.
This story now, is at its end, of Papa Weirisch's life,

18

'how the world has changed since he passed on, with its crime,
                                          pollution, ---
Strife. ----
All we have, are but the memories, of that lifetime long ago,
the places, and the faces, of those people we loved so.
everytime I think of them, it is like a sweet refrain,
God bless each, and every one of them, until we meet again; ---


## DAY TRIP TO MARGATE

We all had a day trip to Margate.
It was August, nineteen thirty three.
I will never forget the excitement!
at the prospect of seeing the sea.

There was 'mum and dad,' 'Winnie, and Harold,'
'Reg and Doll;,' Peter and Stan,
'Aunt Soph, Uncle Vic, 'Cousin Doris,'
'Hal's mum and dad, 'Harry, and Ann!'

Dad hired a Chara to take us,
there we were, all crammed inside,
my old Squeeze box, I took along with me,
to provide music during the ride.

Everyone on the coach were all happy,
we sang going down all the way.
From a blue sky, the sun shone in glory,
and it promised to be a Good Day!

We stopped for a break during the journey,
Out came our Sandwiches, Beer,
Ham, Pickled Onions, Tomatoes,
our Glasses were raised in Good Cheer!

It was time to resume our long journey,
'T'was a long way to Margate On Sea,
Some of our party went missing,
they had sloped off to have a quick, pee!

Back on the coach, we were merry,
some resumed eating their snack,
mum and dad sat in the seats at the front,
Courting couples, they sat at the back.

Everyone joined in the laughter,
as slowly, the coach pulled away,
Once again, I donned the old Squeeze-box,
and I happily, started to play!

When we arrived, 'It was lovely!'
We found a nice spot on the beach,
Harold's dad, disappeared to buy ice-cream,
and we all had a nice cornet each.

The 'Cool breeze from the sea, was most welcome,'
It turned out to be a hot, day.
Dad said, 'give me a tune on your squeeze-box,'
so I once again, started to play.

We all sat around in a circle,
everyone burst into song.
Folk watching from above, threw down Pennie's,
before resuming their stroll on the Prom.

The menfolk, they rolled up their trousers,
for a paddle in the cool, Margate sea,
soon after, the women all followed,
sploshing about and shrieking with glee!

We knew how to enjoy ourselves them days!
Not a miserable face to be seen!
People were then, far more happy,
'More contented, if you know what I mean.

Dad said to mum, 'Ain't it grand, Nell?'
'It's been such a wonderful day!'
'I have never enjoyed meself so much before,'
'It's been smashing, that's all I can say!'

I have never known time pass so quickly,
The sunset glowed red in the sky,
when dad pulled out his watch from his pocket,
'Twas his queue to bid Margate, Goodbye!'

Our coach in the car-park was waiting.
As reluctantly, we all climbed aboard.
'Reg,' 'Doll,' 'Win,' and 'Hal,' were the last to get on,
and in the back seat, they all sprawled!

Once again, I strapped on me old Squeeze-box.
The smoke in the coach, made me cough!
With everyone comfortably seated,
with a grind of the gears, we were off!'

I very soon got everyone singing,
I played till I felt fit to drop!
I carried on playing regardless,
all the way till we had our next stop.

We pulled in at a pub in the country,
It looked charming, lit up from outside!
Making our way to the door of the coach,
'Watch out for the Steps!; my dad cried.

We all had a 'jolly, good nosh up!'
More beer, was consumed on the night.
Someone got on the piano!
And we all came out 'Merry, and Bright!'

d

By the time we arrived back in London,
We were all tired, and ready for bed.
Thinking back too those days of the Thirties,
I must say, 'There's a lot to be said!'

When I'm sitting quiet in my armchair,
I like to stroll down 'Memory Lane!'
There's one thing for certain, I must say,
'We won't see them days back again!'

## THE PENFOLD'S

There were 'five of us kids, in the family.'
My poor mum, she had her hands full.
I was the 'baby of the family,'
the other four, going to school.
'Three brothers, I had, and a sister,'
No wonder, poor mum, looked her age!
Her life, was one big, constant, worry,
trying to feed us, on Dad's meagre wage!

Times were real hard, in the Twenties,
'Patched clothes, was the 'badge of the times,'
the unemployed, hung about on street corners,
'No wonder, there were so many crimes!'
With my poor mother's purse almost empty,
She did not know which way to turn.
For 'There were no hand-outs, in those days,'
Only the 'Rich,' who had money, to burn!

Every week, meant a trip to the 'Pawn shop,'
sighing, 'Oh dear, When will it all end?'
'Why should this life be 'such a worry?'
the answer, she could not, comprehend!'
Though Dad did his best, to support us,
it was, a most difficult task.
Mum nagged him to ask for more money!
but Dad was 'too frightened, to ask.' ---

In those days, the 'Unions, were frowned on!'
the Govnor's had it 'all their own way!'
'What an unjust world it was then, to live in!'
And 'Men got the sack, every day.'
Mum was always hard pushed, come the Thursday,
she did not quite know, What to do!
She mostly relied on the Ragman,
to 'feed our poor body's with stew.

Mum slaved every hour, that God gave her,
No wonder she looked so worn out.
There wasn't a lazy bone in her body,
and for 'all her hard work, 'she got nowt!'
'Five, ragamuffin's, she was blessed with,'
all clamouring for attention, each day,
coming in from the street, with 'Black faces,'
'Torn trousers, drooping socks, from their play.'

In spite of it all, 'How mum loved us!'
she would, not part with 'one single one,'
mum referred to us all as 'Her Potherbs,"
and, 'Everything under the sun!'
Below us, there lived all the Pavey's,
who also had kids of their own,
Squabbling with each other out the garden,
like 'dogs, fighting over a bone!'

Sometimes we all played together,
sharing, our few, precious, toys,
skipping with a length of old clothes-line,
until 'Someone, complained of the noise!'
'Up, slid the sash, corded window,'
Head in curlers, would, 'quickly pop out,'
Warning us all, 'To be quieter,'
till one of us, 'ended up with a clout!'

In our flat, there was never a dull moment,
there was always, activity going on!
Dad would slip in the parlour, unnoticed,
to play Piano, and to give us a song.
Even though we were poor, we were happy,
there were times when mum laughed, till she cried,
like 'When Dad put his foot in the Jerry,'
tears of laughter, she just, could not hide.

Our flat, just like others, had problems.
To mum's horror, she discovered, 'we had mice!'
all the traps that she bought, did not catch them,
after all, 'It was not, very, nice!' ---

Whilst cleaning beneath her old dresser,
she had a considerable scare,
when a mouse, scrambled out of its hiding,
mum 'screamed,' and she 'jumped on a chair!'
Mum and Dad, never usually quarrelled!
they both preferred peace, Bless their Souls,
but when Dad arrived home for his dinner,
mum made him 'block up, all the holes.'

Mum simply adored all her off-spring,
to her, We could do nothing, wrong!
but she must have got fed up with us sometimes,
we were 'under her feet, all day long!'
Like all kids, I was 'very mischievous!'
and sometimes, it earned me a 'Whack,'
like the day she popped out for some shopping,
saying, 'sit there, until I come back!'

I filled up the sink with cold water,
then 'I paddled, which filled me with glee,'
'Sploshing about with excitement,'
making believe 'It was 'Southend on Sea!'
When mum returned, 'By God, she was furious!'
she 'hurriedly lifted me out,'
I had never seen her 'quite so angry,'
which resulted in me, 'getting a clout!' ---

To achieve keeping us all in order,
On the clothes-line, hung mum's 'penny cane!'
If she had to, 'she'd give us a whacking,'
Screaming, 'Now don't you do that again!' ---

As usual, 'Each Saturday morning,'
We all had our small tasks to do!;
It was my job to cut, squares of paper,
to be 'Threaded,' and 'put in the loo!'
Win's was to 'blacklead the fireplace,'
It was 'Stan's job, to 'whiten the hearth.'
'Reg used to clean all my mum's 'knives and forks,'
and, 'Pete's job, was sweeping the path!'
If 'lucky, we might cop a 'ha'penny,'
but 'not often, did one, come our way.'
Mum's 'Ha'pennies, to her, they were precious,'
they were 'needed to live, 'every day.'

We always looked forward to Christmas.
for it filled our young hearts with 'pure joy!'
We 'just could not sleep with excitement,'
at the 'thought' of 'receiving a toy!'
We usually got a 'few pennies,'
an 'orange, apple and nuts,'
including a 'couple of popular games,'
not forgetting of course, 'Comic cuts!'
It meant 'such a lot to us children,'
Still the joy of them days, I recall!,
for 'although mum and dad, were not wealthy,'
'They both did their 'best, for us all!'

We were all made to go to Church Sundays,
to 'Give praise unto our 'Dear Lord!'
Not always, could we give to the collection,
for the money, mum 'could not afford!'
Her 'poor purse was always so empty,'
I felt sorry for her, the 'poor bitch!'
Whilst I was there, I would say in my prayer,
'Oh Dear God, Please make Daddy rich!' ---

There were times, when I felt, 'so hard done by,'
when I saw the toys other kids had.
Broken hearted, I sobbed to my mother,
It was futile, my pleading to Dad!
Mum said, 'Come over here, me Ole, Potherb,'
I immediately did as was bid!
Inside, I was 'seething with sorrow,'
for, 'I was a 'sensitive kid!' ---

'It isn't because we don't love you,'
'You know it's not that, my sweet honey,'
'You could have the 'top brick off the chimney,'
'It's because, we just don't have the money!'
'You should know that if we could afford it,'
'There is 'nothing that we would not give,'
'Than to see our sweet little boy happy,'
'Not just for now ' 'but as long as you live!'

Even though mum and dad, 'they both loved us,'
We were made to do 'What we were told,'
It only took 'one or two wollops,'
after that, 'we were all good as gold!'

What my dear mum lacked in money,
was 'replaced with her undying love,'
though our lives were not 'all milk and honey,'
her 'love and care went hand in glove!'

'Bath night, my poor mother dreaded!'
though to us, it was 'one, round of fun,'
We all had to share the same water,
until, all of us had been done.
Mum worried about 'Ma Pavie's ceiling,'
who complained that 'the water came through,'
She showed mum a 'couple of damp patches,'
and poor mum, would come back feeling blue!

We were given our Friday night jollop!
'Syrup of figs, was the usual trend,'
though we all seemed to 'rebel against it,'
'We all got it down, in the end!'
Mum would 'thump at the lumps in the mattress,'
before 'tucking us up, in our beds'
After saying our prayers, she would 'bid us goodnight,'
as she 'brushed a light kiss on our heads.'
I gazed up at the ring on the ceiling,
which reflected from the 'Paraffin lamp,'
it appeared to show up all the patches,
where the 'inlet of rain, made it damp!'

How mum put up with it all, 'I don't know,'
for 'it was a deplorable place,'
She must have been very strong willed, I should think,
for she 'always put on a brave face.'
I was fumbling with the beads that hung from her neck,
when a 'tear trickled from my mum's eye,'
It filled me with regret to see her upset,
for it 'hurt me to see my mum cry.'

Looking back, like I do, on those days, I once knew,
and 'Thinking of dear mum and dad,'
'Tears fill my eyes, for I now realise,
'The sheer hardship, the poor buggers had!'
As I sit in my chair, at their photo, I stare,
for their 'sweet memory still lingers on,'
In my heart, 'I still grieve,' for it's hard to believe,
that, 'both my dear parents have gone!'
I am now seventy four, to this day, 'I'm still poor,'
'Good fortune somehow's passed me by,'
I don't have to be told, that there's 'no pot of gold,'
not for me, till the 'day that I die.'

# THE VINTAGE YEARS

Looking back the way I do, I can see it all today.
'Gordon Richards' won the Derby, and dad had a bob each way.
'Fred Astaire,' and 'Ginger Rogers' were appearing in 'top Hat,'
and I smoked my first cigarette, from a packet of 'Black Cat.'
That summer I remember well, with its flowers in full bloom,
as a shaft of sunlight filtered through the window of our room.
My father had the wireless on, and I listened to the cricket,
as 'Harrold Larwood, 'in his stride, took wicket after wicket.

'Malcolm Campbell' in his 'Bluebird, sped through water like a
Rocket,
and he returned triumphant, with the record in his pocket.
We listened to the music of the fabulous 'Jerome Kern,'
and a man that they called Hitler, seemed to cause us great concern.
Germany was re-arming as fast as she possibly could,
it was rumoured in the papers, that her tanks were made of wood?
Stanley Baldwin, he stood proudly, outside of Number Ten,
and 'Goodbye Mr Chipps' flowed from the 'Great James Hilton's
pen.'

Great ships were built in dock-yards, on the Tyneside, and the
Clyde,
Skilled hands produced the finest ships which were looked upon
with pride.
The fabulous 'Queen Mary,' in her berth 'Southampton Dock,'
displayed her 'Three, Red Funnels,' and was solid as a rock.
She was 'Queen of the Atlantic,' and we all felt very proud,
where ever this Great liner docked, she always drew a crowd.

Cinemas and theatres, in those days, were all the go,
for the price of a few coppers, you could go and see a show.
There were stars like 'Gertrude Lawrence,' 'Jessie Mathews,' 'Jack
Buchanon,'
'Arthur Askey' Richard Murdock,' -- 'Flannagen and Allen.'

'Max Miller' brought the place down, he was known as 'The Cheeky
Chappie,'
people seemed to love what was called Blue jokes, and he kept the
audience happy. ---
The Successful Musical 'Me and my girl,' in nineteen thirty eight,
came the Cockney song, 'The Lambeth Walk, everybody thought it
great.
People danced it in their homes, it was whistled in the street,
it was a very catchy song, which gave rhythm to your feet.

Unemployment in the thirties, and Industrial decay,
caused misery, and hardship, to millions day by day.
The Prince of Wales, I still recall, was soaking up the sun<
and when the Prince returned from Wales, said 'Something must be
done.'
The poverty in Britain, to this day I still recall,
the past is not forgotten, and a lesson to us all.

The old age pension was ten bob (fifty pence today)
The Unions fought the bosses, for a 'Holiday with Pay.'
The Pawnshops used to flourish and things looked very bleak,
there was of course, The Workhouse, or the 'R.O., - so to speak.
Twas the Bailiff who decided which possessions had to go,
before you got a penny, in those days of long ago.

My mother's Co-op Divi, was a shilling in the pound,
It came in very handy when the holidays came round.
In the burning week of August, to the coast, we used to flood,
where incognito, stalked a man, who was known as 'Lobby Ludd.'
If people thought they spotted him, they would follow him like flies,
if you challenged him correctly, then you could claim your prize.
British people loved their hiking, they left the town in droves,
their knapsacks, carried everything, bar their kitchen sinks and
stoves.
The poorer folk of London, went 'Hop Picking,' down in Kent,
They usually left from London Bridge, 'It was a Great Event.' ---

Telegraph boys, wearing Pillbox caps, rode the streets on their red
bikes.
The thirties was an era, of discontentment, lock-outs, strikes,
It was 'sixpence for a haircut,' fourpence for a shave,'
and 'tuppence for the barber, for the service that he gave.
A new car cost one hundred pounds, or ten pound for a secondhand
banger,
my parents transport was the tram, 'the good old fashion clanger.'
'Fred Perry' retained the Davis Cup, in nineteen thirty four,
and 'nothing over sixpence could be bought in Woolworth's store.'

Capital Punishment for murder,' was the Law in my young day.
To dangle on the hangman's rope, was the price one had to pay.
'Pierpoint was the Hangman.' He'd topped many in his time,
The good thing about Capital Punishment was, 'It seemed to fit the
crime.'

'Oswald Mosley's name appeared, on soot ingrained brick walls,
and I noticed underneath his name, someone had written 'Balls.' ---
The Blackshirts held their meetings at the corner of the street,
and many folk got injured, neath the hooves of horses feet.
Often Vicious fights broke out, and a bloodbath would ensue,
as the mounted Police drew batons, when bricks and bottles flew.

People gasped in horror, as they listened to the news,
of Hitler's Concentration Camps 'Persecution of the Jews.' ---
Whilst Mussolini, the Dictator, in his 'Bumptious, arrogant prime,'
emphatically declared to all, 'That his trains would run on time.' ---
His assault on 'Ethiopia,' caused world wide condemnation,
though we did not lift a finger against this 'aggressive, violation.'

The Spanish Civil War took place, in nineteen thirty six.
I saw their cities being bombed on the Newsreels at the pics.
Heavy casualties grew day by day, as the bombers took their toll,
such tragedy, filled the very hearts, of every living soul. ---

Great Britain had an Empire, we were glorious and free.
Respected by our colonies, in those lands across the sea.
'Queen Mary and King George The Fifth, was loved by one and all,
Their overwhelming popularity, to this day, I still recall.

A 'sea monster,' had been spotted in the beautiful Lochness.
It received 'Maximum Publicity,' by the media of the Press.
People flocked to Scotland in their hope to get a view,
and I have often wondered, 'Was it fictitious?' or 'was it true?' ---

People leaned upon their gates, and rested from their chores,
for the Summers of the thirties, were too hot to stay indoors.
The Winters, they were quite severe, whilst the bitter winds, did
blow.
The unemployed were given jobs, to clear away the snow.

'Picturegoer Weekly,' was a popular magazine.
It depicted all our favourite Stars, that we saw on the screen.
Not forgetting 'Picture Post,' which won our admiration,
with its news and views, of World Affairs, 'Its Gigantic circulation.'
My mother used to read 'John Bull,' she swore 'it was the best,'
as in her chair, she used to sit, to have a well earned rest.

Tommy Farr fought Joe Lousie, 'One of the all time greats.'
they used to call him 'The Brown Bomber,' in the United States.
Our gallant Tommy lost on points, though the verdict, it was tight,
but it was worth getting up at three a.m. to listen to the fight.

It was during the thirties, the 'swing era had arrived,'
It came to no surprise the way it flourished, and survived.
We listened to live music from the big bands of the day,
Dance halls became quite popular, as we danced the night away.
There was 'Henry Hall,' 'Bert Ambrose,' 'Jack Hylton,' 'Harry Roy,'
'Jack Payne,' and 'Billy Cotton,' all filled our hearts with joy.

When our beloved Monarch died, the Prince of Wales became our
King.
We looked forward to prosperity, and new hope that he would
bring.

His love for Mrs. Simpson, he simply could not hide,
and said 'He could not carry on, without her by his side.'
His statement from the Palace, filled our hearts with devastation,
as he broadcast to his people, <u>His Intended Abdication.</u>
Mrs. Simpson as a future Queen, <u>the Government could not condone</u>
and 'His Royal Highness,' the Duke of York, gained succession to
the Throne.

The submarine 'H.M.S. Thetis' on sea trials off Liverpool Bay,
tragically dived to her doom, I'm very sad to say.
This unfortunate disaster, as cruel as it could be,
claimed the lives of several ratings, to the peril of the sea.

I loved to go up London, if my mum could pay the fare,
to explore the Mighty City, 'Piccadilly,' 'Leicester Square.'
This did not happen often, but when it did, 'I jumped for joy,'
'How wonderful life used to be,' when I was just a boy.

The cobbled streets of London rang, beneath the horses hooves,
tall chimneys belched forth acrid smoke, from their soot inlaiden
roofs.
Cherryblossom Bootblacks, could be seen outside each Station,
polishing the boots, and shoes, of the busy population.

City dwellers dodged between the traffic in the street,
the pavements seemed to echo with a million, busy feet.
Flower girls with baskets filled, with violets drenched with dew,
in their flowered hats, and tattered shawls, running noses, cold and
blue.

Clanging trams and weaving taxis, as they darted to and fro,
gruffy voices of Newsvendors, with red faces all aglow.
Dining rooms with steamy windows, horse and cart outside,
savoury smells beneath the grating, permeating far and wide.
All those things I still remember, from those happy days gone by,
as nostalgic memories thus bring forth, a tear within my eye.
I watched the tugs and barges, plough their way along the Thames,
sunbeams danced upon the water, like a million sparkling gems.

Towards the end of a tiring day, I would soon be homeward bound,
still savouring the sights I'd seen, the excitement that I'd found.
As the evening shadows filled the sky, and night began to fall,
City workers making their way home, reduced traffic to a crawl.
The lights of London glittered like the jewels in the Crown,
as beneath the darkened sky above, beat the heart of London Town.

The German Chancellor Herr Hitler, soon became 'Head of the
State,'
then came the Munich Crisis in nineteen thirty eight.
We were issued out with gasmasks, I will never forget that day,
they were lined up on our sideboard, for the 'Imminent affray.' ---
My father joined the A.R.P,' like several hundreds more,
though in our hearts, I think we knew, 'We were not prepared for
war.'

Mr. Chamberlain flew to Munich. 'For Peace, he paved the way,'
and he returned triumphant, 'it was him, who saved the day.' ---
He waved a piece of paper, with a smile upon his face,
with mixed feelings, people cheered him, some expressed their deep
disgrace,
The War had been averted, and people breathed again,
though the stigma of appeasement, forever will remain.

'Murder, Muggins, Rapists,' in those days, were very rare,
you could leave your street door open, where today, you would not
dare.
'Drug addiction,' wasn't heard of, when I was still a lad,
and neither was pornography, 'I think the world's gone mad. ---
We're too influenced by others, 'I think it is a shame,'
'We shall have to see what we can do, to save Old England's Name.'

The Second World War broke out, in 'Nineteen thirty nine.'
On that fateful Sunday morning, the weather was divine.
It almost seemed impossible that Britain was at war,
twas the ending of an era, like the closing of a door.
The thirties I'll remember, its laughter, and its tears,
with all that transpired in my life, throughout those Vintage Years.'

# A BRIEF ENCOUNTER

I was speaking to an Atheist, whom I met the other day.
Twas intriguing just to listen to the things he had to say.
We spoke about Religion, and of 'how the world had changed,'
though at times, we begged to differ, as opinions were exchanged.
I don't usually discuss Religion, it's an unwise thing to do,
but in a friendly manner, we discussed our Points of view.
I expressed my firm belief in God, that my faith in him was strong,
for I pray to him for guidance, when things in life, go wrong.
For God, is my salvation, in him, I place my trust,
Creator of all life on earth, till we return to Dust!

We conversed about old churches, of their 'dwindling, congregation,'
of the 'beautiful things inside them,' which commanded, admiration!
He informed me, he'd seen many, on his travels, far and wide,
and although he was an atheist, he always went inside.
He quoted me a verse or two, from the Bible, which he'd read,
and of 'Why he was an atheist,' and this, is what he said.

'My church is all around me,' as I step out of my door,
'I can see it, smell it, hear it, how could I wish for more?'
'My God, Den, is nature! Believe me when I say,'
'I find her 'irresistible, and all powerful, in her way!'
'My Altar, is my bird-stand, which I replenish every morn,'
'Oh the pleasure, those birds give me, as they hop about my lawn.'
'I've a great love for old churches, though an atheist, I be,'
'for churches, mosques and synagogues, are a marvel, I agree!'
'They contain the most beautiful works of art,' that human hands,
could fashion!' Such Masterpieces in stone, and wood, deeply fills
me with 'Great Passion.' ---

'All the world's many Gods, were invented of course by Man,'
That is a fact, my dear old friend, Dispute it, if you can!'
'No religious person will agree that what I've said is true,'
'But whether you share my firm belief, is entirely up to you!'
'When one looks at the Lebanon where 'Christian, Arab, Jew,'
'are killing each other in the name of God, 'What Freud once said, 'Is
true!'

'Christians give their thanks to God, from whom all blessings flow,'
'But they don't thank him for earthquakes, or volcanoes, Oh dear no.'
'The Christians call it an 'Act of God,' - Some God, Den, I must say,'
'When the aftermath is over, they fall on their knees to pray!'
'In fact, 'I am a Buddhist,' which is a way of life,'
'It gives me peace and comfort, and alleviates my strife.'

'I don't believe in all that nonsense as regards the 'Virgin Birth,'
'I consider it a 'lot of rot,' for what the story's worth!' ---
'Neither the feeding of 'ten thousand' with two loaves and five
                                                        fishes,'
'If God performed such miracles, then I'll give him my best wishes.'
'You've only got to think of all those people killed by war,'
'Famines and starvation, God's a lot to answer for.'
'The Heart-ache, and the suffering, the hell we all went through.'
'Hitler's Concentration Camps, Annihilation of the Jews,'
'All those wicked, evil deeds, God did not want to know,'
'He shut his eyes to all of them, yet, still to church they go.'
'If aer I reach those 'Pearly Gates, in Heaven' up above,'
I will have a lot to say to him, 'This so called, God of Love.' ---

I respectfully reminded him, that 'as far as I recall,'
'But for our Loving Father, life would not exist, at all.'
That Wars have always taken place, ever since the world began,
you 'cannot blame the Lord for that, but the evilness of man.'
The things this man had said to me, had 'given me food for thought,'
But my Christian upbringing had proved 'too strong,' with the things
that I'd been taught.. ---

Though I listened to all he'd had to say, he probably, thought me
                                                        odd,
I still feel the presence in my heart, of my 'Loving, Father, 'God.'
I hoped I did not give offence, if I did, 'he gave no sign,'
for 'I respected his beliefs,' and he respected mine.
With our conversation over, we parted, 'best of friends,'
I trust this has been of 'interest' for 'here my story ends.'

# YE OLDE ANTIQUE SHOP

What strange magic, little shop,
guides my footsteps and bids me stop?
You haven't the splendour of Aladdin's cave,
or the simple beauty of a stone-flagged nave
yet, in your dim interior, I sense,
an air of sacredness and tolerance.

Perhaps past owners of the things I see,
pass judgement on such as me.
probing my soul, as though to measure,
my worthiness to own their treasure.
What stories could this treasure tell,
of bygone centuries and what befell;
I wonder.

Did this ivory cross once grace a Nun?
or robber flourish this brass-bound gun?
Surely a Dutchman fashioned this old delft plate,
and seaman's knife, this ship of State?
The dish of coins, The Roman lamps,
Necklace of Coral, album of stamps.
Print of Trafalgar, (wonderful sight,)
and visored helmet of some proud Knight.
The rapier with slender blade,
the Chinese Buddha, carved in jade.
The old oak chest, the warming pan,
the sundial and the fragile fan,
the musical box, and Zulu spear,
each have a story I'd love to hear.

From the North, South, East, and West,
to this little shop, they've come to rest.
Owned by people of every creed,
some, may be rich, others in need.
In existence throughout the ages,
when time was writing History's pages.
No wonder this place has a sacred air,
for spiritual forms must hover there,
and if I take a treasure home,
I'm sure I will not walk alone.

## A TREE

Though poor am I, yet poorer still is he,
who looks, yet sees, no beauty in a tree.
How ill doth man compare, with yonder monarch standing there.
Majestic, and aloof, deep rooted as a rock,
untouched by tempests which have tried to mock.

By each gnarled root, each fairy leaf is fed,
to form a verdant green, about his mighty head.
With arms uplifted to the evening sky,
each passing breeze, becomes a fervent sigh.

Does he implore the heavens to impart,
a love of Nature to the human heart.

## NINETEEN THIRTY NINE

Once again, a world of madness, hate and spitefulness abounds,
Love and beauty, joy and laughter, melt like snow as gunfire sounds.
Woods so full of lovers memories, birds, flowers, and grassy glades,
blasted, shattered, blood be spattered,
for Man <u>must</u> use the guns he's made.

## AD VER SITY

The tramp sat by his smouldering fire,
for the night was cold and dark,
and the flickering firelight showed the lines,
where care had left its mark.

He thought of days so long ago,
when he was young and gay,
of the friends he had in hundreds,
how his money paid their way.

How times had changed, no friends he knew,
and with these thoughts, his longing grew,
for friends that were.

His ballroom ceiling now the sky,
his chandelier, the moon on high,
the pine trees, black against the noon,
seemed like the walls of that great room.
Then suddenly, the girl who died,
came through the gloom right to his side,
and gently led him by the hand,
into her far far better land.

# MAGIC VIOLIN

Whilst passing by an antique shop,
your beauty bid my footsteps stop!
My adoration knew no bounds,
What a bargain for just fifty pounds.
It is not too difficult to understand,
you were fashioned by a Craftsman's hand.
It was plain to see, you were made with love,
as you stared at me, from your shelf above.
Nestled in your open case,
put an eager smile upon my face.
I did not have to count to ten,
I had to have you, there and then!

Oh magic, little Violin,
firmly tucked beneath my chin,
is it possible for you to know,
Just how much I love you so!
As my nimble fingers caress your strings,
Oh the utter joy, your sweet voice brings.
So expressly, your sweet notes flow,
with each glide of my slender bow.
I can make you laugh, I can make you cry!
and the hardest heart, you can make it sigh!
How sad this lonely world would be!
if void of simple melody!
Like the rarest jewel my eyes behold,
to me, you're worth much more than gold.

I'm no Paganini, and you're no Strad,
but without you I would feel sad!
You are my life! my soul within!
Oh magic, little Violin.

# MEMORIES OF THE HIGH STREET

I can see it all now, as my sweet memories flow,
the old fashioned High Street of old Walthamstow.
Stalls lined the gutter both sides of the street,
up and down the old market, trod thousands of feet.
Looking back with nostalgia, my mind still recalls,
the 'naphtha-flare lamps,' as they hissed on the stalls.
It was crowded with shoppers, on Saturday night,
and all the shop windows were 'blazing with light.'
Outside of their shops, the butchers would tout,
'Buy, buy, buy, buy,' they would holler and shout.
To auction off meat in those days was the trend,
to save it from hanging around the weekend.
By the end of the evening, their prices would drop,
and by the way of a bonus 'a bit on the top!'
They knew in their wisdom, that the meat would not keep,
so that was the reason, they sold it off cheap!

The old German butchers, did us all a good turn,
as inside of their shop, gleamed a 'bright, coppered urn.'
It was filled with 'Hot Savs, and Steaming, Pease Pudd,'
and for only a penny, it tasted 'real good!'
Each mouthful I ate, I enjoyed a great deal,
for it was a most 'tasty and succulent meal.'

Not far from the butchers, was the 'Sally arcade,'
and on the street corner, the 'Sally-an played.'
In their quaint little bonnets, tied up in a bow,
they handed out 'War-Cry,' as you passed to and fro.
Oh how I loved their glorious Band,
and their wonderful hymns, which sounded so grand.

Many a time came the poor shuffling feet,
of the Ex-Serviceman's Band, as they trailed down the street.
The 'First World War Songs, were the tunes that they played,
in their tunics of blue, and their tattered Gold Braid.
When you gave them a copper, a gruff voice would say,
'Gawd Bless Yer Guv,' as they went on their way.

Further along, stood the old coughdrop man,
who dribbled brown sugar in his deep copper pan.
With his added ingredients, to make it taste good,
it smelt so delicious like a good, cough sweet should.
It was kneaded and rolled on a marble topped slab,
with his 'humorous, patter, and gift of the gab!'
As the crowd all pushed forward to have a good look,
he would then flop it over, a kind of steel hook.
It was 'twisted, platted, knotted, and roped,'
it was marvellous really, the way that he coped.
After he'd finished the 'flips and the flops,'
they went into a Press, and 'Out came the Drops!'

If a 'hot drink you fancied, on a cold winter's night,
the 'Sarsaparilla Stall,' was a most welcome sight!
At a penny per glass, the man did a good trade,
and it warmed the old tum, for the penny that you paid.
the stalls in those days, they were out until ten,
'What a difference today?' to what it was then!

The Walthamstow Palace, was one of our treats,
thick was the carpet, and plush were the seats.
From the top of the Gods, we looked down on the stalls,
on a big sea of hats, my mind, still recalls.
Up drifted the music, and the smell of cigars,
as we happily sat there, with our dear old ma's.
So excited we were, as the lights, they went low,
it was 'up with the curtain, and on with the show!'

The Old Truant School, where the bad boys abode,
was right at the bottom of Palmeston Road.
Lined up in the playground, they all looked so glum,
'The poor little buggers,' said my dear old mum.
They stood to attention in columns of four,
the site is now occupied by the new Woolworth's Store.

I remember the joy that it used to give me,
as I gazed at the counters, which filled me with glee.
All those long years ago, when I was a small boy,

when for only a 'tanner,' I came out with a toy!
Christmas at Woolworths filled my heart with delight,
with its 'last minute shoppers on Christmas Eve night.
With a bob in my pocket, which was all that I had,
it paid for a present, for my dear mum and dad!
With my purchase completed, 'out, I would come,'
to make my way home, to my 'darling old mum.'

I remember the church, with its 'tall graceful spire,'
each time that I looked, it seemed ;higher and higher!'
The 'Grand Central Library,' which is still used today,
next door to the Baths, where the kids used to play.
Shrieks of delight, echoed from the inside,
and 'Both of those buildings,' were looked on with pride.

Just beyond Willow Walk, stood the man with his scales,
with its swinging wood seat, and its 'polished brass rails.'
I can hear his voice now crying, 'Thirteen stone eight,'
as he wrote out a ticket and put down your weight.
The stallholders humour, filled me with delight,
the 'Backbone of High Street' on a Saturday night!
These old cockney characters have now but all gone,
but the memory of them, in my heart, 'lingers on.'
The ghost of their voices, still ring in my ears,
from those days, 'long ago,' with my laughter and tears.

The 'cheap jacks' that swore they could cure all your ills,
with their 'small screw of paper, which contained a few pills.'
They reeled of their patter, as you pressed round the stall,
and 'whatever your ailment, they had cures for them all!'

My Saturday treat, was still yet to come,
when I went into 'Manzes' with my dear old mum.
Perched on a bench, with a table well scrubbed,
proved to be a 'tight squeeze' as our shoulders they rubbed.
I enjoyed every morsel of the food that I ate,
as I spooned up the liqueur with relish, from my plate.
With satisfied tummies, we made our way out,
then 'into the Cock for mum's half a pint, Stout!

As I waited outside, my comic I'd scan,
seeking warmth from the brazier of the 'Old Chestnut Man.'

I remember with affection, the market I loved,
as 'Down its long street' we 'pushed, and we shoved,'
Those 'cold winter nights,' when our hands and feet froze,
and the 'Dewdrop that trickled from our cold runny nose.
The way that its altered, leaves me feeling, 'quite sad,'
when I think of those wonderful days we once had!
The High Street today, it just 'isn't the same,'
and the only thing left from those days, is its name!
In my heart, I still cling to its 'Sweet Memory,"
and that 'Wonderful era,' that meant 'So much to me.'

# GRANDMA PENFOLD

This is the story of my dear Grandma Pen.
who outlived the lifespan (three score years and ten.)
I still picture her now, as she was in those days,
with her sweet smiling face, and her loveable ways.
My Grandfather loved her from the moment they met,
it was love at first sight, just like Scarlet, and Rhet.
They were both very happy from the day that they wed,
for my grandad, he worshipped the ground that she tread.
She bore 'seven sons' and was proud of them all,
whom in turn idolised her, from the time they could crawl.
Gran often gave thanks to the dear Lord above,
for bestowing on her, seven sons she could love.

When dad sent me round with a note for my gran,
the first thing she'd say was, 'How is my dear Stan?' ---
What a welcome she'd give as I walked through the door,
with a 'hug and wet kiss,' as my feet left the floor.
Her hands helped me off with my coat, and my cap,
and the next thing I knew, --- I was on my gran's lap.
Gran knew that my journey had been a long trek,
as my small fingers fumbled the beads round her neck.

Gran would tell me a story of when she was young
Of the popular songs, which in those days were sung.
The East End of London, with its cobble stone streets,
hansome cabs, - and horse buses, - with their hard, wooden seats.
The soot laden roofs, the grimy brick walls,
the Variety artists, - and the Old Music Halls.
The flower girls, wearing their flowered, straw hats,
the bootblacks, the sweeps, - and the street urchin brats.
The cold of the winter, - the peasouper fog,
and the locals that came in for their drop of grog.
Drunkenness was the thin part of the wedge,
and many a man in his time, signed the pledge.
The match girls that sweated for 'Bryant and Mays,'
and of how hard life was, for a crust in them days.

Gran said, 'that her father, was a very kind man.'
Hard working, honest, and who loved my dear gran.
Well known in the City, and respected by all,
as my gran told me everything she could recall.
With the siege of Sidney Street,' fresh in her mind,
gran recalled all those days which she'd now left behind.
As I listened to the history which filled my young ears,
gran's far away look, filled her blue eyes with tears.

When the Thames got froze over, gran didn't think twice,
for she walked across it, ' So thick was the ice.' ---
Gran told me she was a daredevil them days,
a fete that won my admiration and praise.
Silk Weavers were well known in grandmother's time,
when she was a young girl, and still in her prime.
The Silk weaving trade, was then at its height,
and special windows were built to let in the light.
Though a skilled craft it was, they worked for low pay,
and the cottages they lived in, are still standing today.

Gran's parents were Publicans back in those days,
when 'Jack the Ripper' stalked London, and 'Marie Lloyd' all the
craze.
Her parents were up at the first crack of dawn,
serving 'hot rum and coffee,' four a.m. in the morn.
That was their busiest time of the day,
till the customers dwindled, and went on their way.
The work - it was hard, and the hours they were long,
and the beer in those days, though cheap, was quite strong.
Pewter tankards were very popular then,
and kept spotlessly clean, by my dear grandma Pen.
Silver sand was the secret to give them a shine,
and the ale from those tankards, tasted really divine.
Though drinking was frowned on, and looked on as sin,
the ladies still longed for their tot of neat gin.

A screw of tobacco was the call of the day,
and Clay pipes if requested, were given away.
Sometimes they'd ask for a small pinch of snuff,
which they sniffed up their nostrils, until they'd had enough.
Twas all part of the service in those days gone by,
for it was on their custom, that they had to rely.

They did a good dinner, at sixpence per head,
'Good value for money,' -- the customers said.
A cut of roast beef, or mutton, with veg,
on a plate that was covered, and filled to the edge.
'How can that pay you?' -- said gran to her dad.
'Only sixpence per dinner, they must think we've gone mad.'
'Ah, said her dad, with a nod, and a wink,
'It's not what they eat dear, -- 'it the ale that they drink.' ---

The height of the summer, brought with it, the flies,
The streets, they were smelly, as the heat seemed to rise.
The aroma of horse dung, pervaded the air,
gran said that the stench was at times, hard to bear.
My gran loved a picnic, and off they would go,
to Whipps Cross in the country, which my dear gran loved so.
they would get brown as berries, being out there all day,
and coming home on the brake, -- they would sing all the way.

When gran moved to Walthamstow (Hazelwood Road,)
for a number of years, it became her abode.
It was all country then, with 'field, stream, and farm,'
with long winding lanes, captivated with charm.
From a yard in St James Street, the horse buses ran,
'where they stopped at the Standard,' said my dear ole gran.
Out stepped the passengers in their Sunday best,
whilst they sponged down the horses, and gave them a rest.

The construction of the Railway, my gran remembered well.
From Liverpool Street, to Chingford, was the tale she used to tell.
It cut straight through the marshes, and people used to wave,
Gran said 'It was a blessing, with the time it used to save.'
Gran remembered the time when they started to build,

the 'Lord Palmerston Pub,' where once stood a big field.
Twas 'a quick cut to Marsh Street, ' my gran used to say.
Oh how things have changed? since it was in gran's day.---

Gran's final move was Leyton, where she lived down Vicarage
Road,
How the poor old cart horse struggled, with the burden of its load.
Listening to my dear old gran, Oh how my memories flow,
who slipped my hand a coin, or two, when time for me to go.
I must confess my darling gran, she had a heart of gold,
Oh how I missed her when she died, at 'Ninety six years old..' ---

# CHRISTMAS TODAY

'It's not like how it used to be,' - you often hear folk say,
'By the time I've finished shopping, I'm worn out by Christmas day.'
'What with hunting round for presents, and wondering what to buy,'
and paying through the nose for them, 'with prices so sky high,'
'Me poor ole feet, are killing me, from traipsing round the shops,'
'What with people pushing and shoving, The aggravation, never
                                                      stops.'
'All the Stalls, - they look alike, with the same old blooming trash,'
'When I see things that I really want, ' 'I can't afford the cash.' ---

'I won't put up with this next year, --- 'I'll knock it on the head,'
'By the time I've done my shopping, --- 'I'm so tired, --- 'I want my
                                                      bed.'
'I'm only buying for the kids, and 'that's my blinking lot,'
'It's ridiculous to carry on, spending money you've not got.'
'I'm fed up to the eyebrows, as up and down, I roam,'
'If it wasn't for the shopping, --- 'I would have stayed at home.' ---
'I mooched around in Woolworths, for presents for the boys,'
'I didn't know what to buy them, --- 'Oh, the price of childrens toys:'
-

'I've bought mince pies and sausage rolls, 'a pudding, and a cake,'
'It's not worth the aggravation of the time they take, to make.'
'I've nearly spent my Christmas Club, --- 'It don't take long to go,'
'I'm down now to my last few quid, --- 'What I'll do then? --' I don't
                                                      know! ---
'It don't seem much like Christmas, - 'I don't like it anymore,'
'The shops, - they shut up early, - and the stalls, pack up by four.' ---
'You never see a smiling face, -- 'everybody's in a hurry,'
'to catch the shops before they close, -- 'Oh, is it worth the worry?' --
'It wasn't like that years ago, --- 'they were open then, till late,'
'Christmas Eve, I'll never leave my house, at least, - till half past
                                                      eight.'
'The shops would still be open, till 'eleven o'clock at night,' ---
'If they had to work those hours today, --- 'they would die of
                                                      blooming fright.'

'It's not like the dear old High Street, -- 'the market'ts not the same,'
'The atmosphere's no longer there, - 'Aint it a blooming shame?' ---
'Every year, the stuff goes up, 'It fair makes me feel sick,'
'What with the Telly - Ads every day, -- 'It does get on your wick.'
'I'm browned off before it gets here, -- 'Every year's the blinking
                                                                        same,'
'Today, -- 'It's too commercialised, -- 'It's the telly, - that I blame.' ---
'I suppose when it's all over, -- 'All we'll hear about are Sales,'
'When all the rubbish shops can't sell, - they'll shove it on their rails.'
'I wonder if it's worth it? -- all the bother, and the fuss,'
'What with lugging back the shopping, 'n waiting hours for the bus.' -
'N, look at what it costs yer - 'Everything today's so dear,'
'No wonder people say, -- Thank God, - 'It's only once a year.' ---

'I aint forgotten last year, - 'We were all down with the flu'
'Stuck in bed all over Christmas, - and queuing for the loo.' ---
'We couldn't eat our dinner, -- 'What a waste of blooming food,'
'And what with dad, with his diarrhoea, -- 'He was 'in a right old
                                                                        mood.' ---
'Never known a Christmas like it, -- 'I was almost near to tears,'
'Even the nuts were rotten, -- 'they must have been last year's.' ---
'those we did eat, weren't much good, - and the 'ole man broke his
                                                                        teeth,'
'Then he took it out on the poor ole cat, -- 'He said, 'it was a thief.'
'He'd caught it on the table, sniffing round the few remains,
'Piss Orf,' - you thieving sod,' - he cried, - and clobbered it for its
                                                                        pains!
The oranges were bitter, and the apples, 'they were hard,' ---
The ole girl was none too happy, - 'Cause I didn't send a card.' ---

Down our street on Christmas night, - 'It's as quiet as quiet could be,'
'They sit there in their darkened rooms, -- 'Gawping at 'T.V.! ---
Though most of it is rubbish, and they've seen it all before,
'they're all in bed by 'half past ten, --- 'Oh, blimey, what a bore.' ---
'Our lot's not much better,-- 'All they want to do is sleep,'
'They've got no life in them today, -- 'It's enough to make one
                                                                        weep.' ---
'By the time it gets to five o'clock, - 'they're screaming for their tea,'

'Plastic ham, with beetroot, - and a stick of celery,' ---
'Then they pull their crackers, and don their paper hats,'
'They act like little children, - 'Oh, it does give me the rats,' ---
They adjourn into the parlour, -- and, 'On goes the blinking Telly,'
leaving me to do the clearing up, - 'Do they help? - 'Not on your
                                                             nelly.' ---

'Years ago when I was young, -- 'we always had a party,'
'The people - they were different then, - 'they were all more
                                          gay and hearty
'Come on Dad, - 'Piano,' - my mother used to say, --
'Each one in turn, would give a song, - 'And all night, - Dad would
                                                             play.' --
'Nower days, they're all like zombies, '- 'They don't know they're
                                                             alive,'
'All they do, - is 'eat and sleep, - 'it's a wonder they survive.' ---
'It's nothing like it used to be, as it was in my young day,'
'I blame the television, - 'that is all I've got to say.' ---
'People too, have changed, -- 'They're greedy now, - All they want, is
<u>more and more,</u>' ---

'It will n ever be the same again, - like it was <u>Before the War</u>.' ---
'As I look back on reflection, of 'How good, they used to be,' ---
'With sadness, I must tell you,' --- '<u>they mean nothing more to me</u>.'
'There's one more thing I'd like to say, - 'If Christmas's survive?' ---
'Thank goodness the way they are today, - that I'm nearly 75.'

# TASTELESS

'How difficult today, to buy a 'tasty, bit of cheese?'
and I'm not the type of fella, that you'd say, was hard to please.
It's just like eating plastic, and there isn't any flavour,
in the 'good old days,' it tasted good and was something you could
'savour.'
It's a 'let down,' when you buy it, and it varies week by week.
folk say, 'I've lost my sense of taste, but I haven't blooming cheek.

It's the same, I find with 'bacon,' it looks nice in the pack,
sometimes I buy streaky, or else, 'a bit of back.'
I used to like it in a sandwich, but 'that was long ago,'
today, I find it 'tasteless,' what they do with it, 'I don't know.'
It shrivels up when it's in the pan, and it 'always seems to stick,'
and the 'smell when it is cooking, it 'makes me feel, 'quite sick.'
When I used to be a lad, it used to be a treat
now after a few days in the fridge, 'it smells like sweaty feet.'

I was partial to a 'bit of ham,' but it's 'not the same no more,'
it's 'either sweaty, or downright wet,' and 'that's about the score.'
Whenever I buy a bit today, 'I seem to come unstuck,'
for to get a bit that's 'tasty,' it's a matter of 'pot luck.'

Corned beef, is not so good today, whatever brand you buy.
it's more fatty, than it used to be, and 'I always find it dry.'
It was worth buying years ago, but 'sadly not today,'
it's 'not a patch on what it was,' 'I don't care what, they say.'
Even spam was better in the war, it 'always tasted good,'
if I could only buy the same today, 'my goodness, yes, I would.'

As for a 'decent sausage,' 'I haven't found one yet,'
I tried a pound the other day, and 'much to my regret.'
I find that when I fry them, 'they nearly always burst,'
it's either because I do something wrong,
Or else, I'm blinking cursed.'
I find them 'boring' anyway, irrespective of their grade,
The 'Germans could teach us a thing, or two, of 'how they should be
made.'

It's the same with 'wafer crackers,' 'they're just like eating straw,'
I loved them with a bit of cheese, but 'I won't buy them, no more.'
'Jacobs, Crawfords,' 'McVities,' I think, I've tried them all,
I've been so disappointed, it 'really gets my gall.'

'Fish and chips,' are on my list, it 'grieves me so to say,'
the chips were 'limp and soggy,' which I bought the other day.
The fish, was mostly 'batter,' and it wasn't very white,'
and the 'oil which they'd been cooked in,' I could taste with 'every
                                                                bite.'
It 'repeated on me after, 'time and time again.'
I enjoyed it 'not one little bit,' but 'who am I to complain?'

I once enjoyed a bit of 'beef,' in the good old days gone by,
but 'it worries me to eat it now,' and 'can you wonder why?'
I really don't know what to think, it is 'safe now,' some folk say,
I debate now, 'should I chance a bit?' Or 'will I rue the day?'
Once upon a time, I used to love a 'savaloy,'
They 'tasted good, with soft peas-pudd,' when I was still a boy.
Today, they're 'nothing like the way they always used to be,'
They're an 'apology,' for a savaloy, 'I must say, 'Believe you me.'
Faggots, were 'delightful,' 'oh how my memories flow,'
'What I wouldn't give to have one now,' 'but that was years ago.'

'Mustard pickle' is another thing, I regret, to have to say,
'What on earth have they gone and done with it? I just throw it
                                                                away.'
It's either bitter or too sweet, but 'why?' that is the question,'
and after I have eaten it, 'I get a bout of indigestion.'

Have you ever tried to open a jar of 'pickle,' 'beets,' or 'jam?'
'Oh what a blinking job it is, 'I always curse and damn.'
The opener doesn't somehow seem to grip the blooming lid,'
the 'blinking, thing kept 'slipping off,' no matter what - I did.
'Why are they hard to open,' that's what I, would like to know,
'Ole well folks, I have had my moan,' 'and now it's time to go,'
'Bye bye ' ---

# LIFE WITH FATHER

'It's one bloody thing after another,' groaned my Dad.
And I've never seen father, so quite, hopping mad.'
The postman had just popped our mail through the door,
and the 'heavy electric bill; was the last straw!

'Just look at it Nell!' cried my dad, as mum froze.
as he 'thrust the unwanted bill, under her nose.'

Holding his head, he looked 'filled with despair,'
then, perused it again, when he'd sunk in his chair.
All you could hear, was the 'tick of the clock,'
as he silently sat there, 'absorbing the shock!'

The offending account was for 'twenty five, bob!'
And the sooner he saw the back of it, 'good job.'
Dad complained that he'd told us, till he was sick and tired,
to 'switch off the lights,' when they 'were not required!'
We had all got the blame, including poor mum,
for the bill he'd received, which was 'such a large sum!'

After having his grumble, he was 'up like a shot,'
and 'reduced all the light bulbs, to 'seventy five watt.'
We noticed the difference being used to bright lights,
and of course being winter, with its 'lengthy dark nights.'
For several nights after, we 'suffered the gloom,'
as the 'dull light cast shadows,' round our 'uncosy room.'
Dad said, 'in the future, this would have to suffice,'
and for 'being extravagant,' 'we all paid the price!'

Being a Thursday, to make matters worse,
There 'wasn't a penny,' 'left in poor mother's purse.'
She knew she would soon, need a 'penny for the gas,'
'Oh the curse that it was! being short of hard cash!'

The situation demanded that 'she'd have to ask dad,'
for the 'loan of two bob,' and 'it made her feel bad!'
She dreaded the moment, knowing what Dad was like,
as he headed for the door, with his 'faithful old bike!'

Mum knew that she couldn't put it off for 'much longer!'
as 'her need for some cash,' became stronger and stronger.'

Crossing her fingers, she made her request
She explained that 'by Thursday, she was always hard pressed.'

Diving into his pocket, Dad pulled out a bob,
Having to plead for some money, almost made my mum sob.
She detested the thought of having to borrow,
and, 'knowing full well,' 'a deduction would follow!'
Whatever Dad loaned her, was 'paid back in full,'
It was stopped from her housekeeping, 'That was Dad's rule.'
It 'meant robbing Peter,' To 'Pay back to Paul,'
for the 'little, it left her, 'was indeed, very small!'
'You'll have to make do Nell on this,' cried my dad.
though mum knew he'd got more, than he told her, he had.

The 'hardship endured, throughout her long life,'
She 'did not deserve it,' for she was a 'good wife!'
'Hard working caring, my mum loved us all,'
and her 'sweet disposition to this day, I recall.'
'Self sacrifice, poverty, seemed to go 'hand in glove,'
What my mum 'lacked in finance,' she made up in her love.'
Her 'sweet loving memory' in my heart will remain!'
Until 'that great day!' when I'll meet her again.'

# THE WILLING HORSE

With the memories come the tears,
as I reminisce those bygone years.
Tears of sorrow, tears of joy,
dog-eared cigarette cards, a broken toy!
Hand-me-down clothes, which had seen better days,
quick to be punished, slow to be praised.
Running errands for all and sundry,
dreading going to school on Monday.
The humiliation of being poor
my envy of the kid next door.
Life was hard indeed for some,
especially for my dear old mum.

To find the rent, to pay our way,
living from hand to mouth each day.
My poor ole mum when times were hard,
did weaving for two-pence, per yard.
Sitting there, I can see her now,
slumped over the table, dabbing her brow.
'Oh what a life!' she used to say,
'all this to earn a crust each day.'
With gnarled hands, and fingers sore,
each twitch of the cottons, a tedious bore.
At times she heaved a weary sigh,
as each laborious hour dragged by.
though exhausted, she still battled on,
through the daylight hours, till the moonlight shone.

'I've done enough!' my mum would say,
'tomorrow is another day'....

Every day it was the same,
'Pegs and Weaving,' Out it came!
She used to work every hour God gave,
till in the end, she became its slave.
Determination, she did not lack,
as she tried to straighten her aching back.
Like an ever turning wheel to treddle,
my mum deserved a blinking medal.


## THE STORY OF MY LIFE

I was born on the eighth of February, in nineteen twenty four,
in a way, I was a burden, for my parents were so poor.
They could well have done without me, just another mouth to feed,
as I suckled at mum's flowing breast, to satisfy my need.
My earliest recollection of my entry to this world,
was a teapot whizzing past my head, which my angry father hurled.
It appears I robbed him of his sleep, I'd kept him up all night,
he could stand my cries no longer, and he threw it out of spite.
It helped relieve his temper, as I whimpered in my cot,
and the first thing that had come to h and, was my mother's China
                                                        pot.
She never forgave him, so I'm told, it broke my mother's heart,
the severity of his action, nearly caused them both to part.

My parents had a sweetshop, it was in Bristol Park Road,
I was still quite young when they moved away, to their humble new
                                                        abode.
It was Leyton, where I first grew up, in my early childhood days,
it was all my father could afford, on the wage he earned at Brays.
I went to school in Capworth Street, when I was five years old,
where discipline, was very strict, and one did as they were told.
The first few days at my new school, I longed for my dear mother,
as the teacher stood with chalk in hand, and a long cane in the other.
I was a rather delicate child, and was always home from school
so my mother spoilt me rotten, I was wrapped in cotton wool.
I had a heart condition, which excluded me from drills,

poor mum was everlasting forking out for Doctor's bills.
We moved back to dear old Walthamstow, in nineteen thirty two,
we lived in Pembar Avenue, twas my mother's dream come true.
I adored the house we lived in, with its sunny, spacious room,
and we had a pretty garden, with a lilac tree in bloom.
I went to school in Blackhorse Road, which was not far from our
home,
where in its asphalt playground, round and round, I used to roam.

I always was a loner, never boisterous, or wild,
my favourite pastime, was my pen, - I was a studious child.
I loved composing verses and poems, that would rhyme,
the other kids would say to me, 'What a boring waste of time.'
It always made me happy, and made me feel content,
to while away the many, many hours, that I spent.
Whilst the other kids were running about, and playing in the street,
'I was writing Poems,' Oh yes, sheet after sheet, after sheet. ---
The magic of the written word, fascinated me no end,
and hidden voices from within, somehow, became my friend.

I had an ear for music, it filled my heart with joy,
I taught myself the accordion, when I was still a boy.
The passing of my Grandad, was how it came about,
for I took down his accordion, when my mum and dad were out.
I fiddled with the buttons, and in no time at all,
I could play the 'National Anthem,' which today, I still recall.
Mum and dad caught me red-handed, it made them both annoyed,
but when I played 'God save the King,' -- my mum was overjoyed.
'From this day on, it's yours' she said. 'You can have it with my
blessing,'
How I mastered it so quickly, always kept my parents guessing.
'It's obviously a gift,' said mum, as happily she vowed,
that 'If Grandad was alive today, Oh wouldn't he be proud.' --
In the end I could play anything, for I progressed every day,
I won a competition, and 'six quid came my way.
When I first learned to play it, I was just eight years of age,
my friends came in to listen, and the garden was my stage.

'Oh what a clever boy you are,' - the neighbours used to say,
'I bet your mum and dad are proud,' -- 'Who taught you to play?' ---
On the third day of September, in nineteen thirty nine,
we learned that Britain was at War, and chills ran down my spine.
I had turned fifteen years old by then, my childhood days had
                                                        passed,
I must say that between the Wars, those years had gone so fast.
By the time that I was twenty, my heart was filled with pride,
I had passed an audition for E.N.S.A., - and toured countrywide.
I played the camps, and factories, in hospitals, round the wards,
in 'Garrison Theatres,' and in fields, on muddy boards.
Never was I so happy, as when rehearsing for a show,
as from my talented fingers, sweet music, used to flow.

I was exempt from Military Service, I was registered as Grade Four,
I felt sad to be rejected, in our struggle to win the War.
I had brothers in the Forces, both serving overseas,
it played upon my conscience, which I thought would never ease.
That's the reason I joined E.N.S.A. being medically unfit,
it made me feel in some small way, that I helped to do my bit. ---

When that wicked War had ended, it was nineteen forty five,
those of us who lived to see the end, were so lucky to survive.
I met a girl, and married her, at the age of twenty three,
and although we had no children, we were happy as could be.
We had to share her parents house, we had two rooms upstairs,
we eventually moved to Harlow, which proved costly, in rent and
                                                        fares.
We stayed there for about three months, we were far from happy
                                                        there,
her parents said, we could come back, our rooms were still to spare.
So back to Walthamstow we came, feeling very much relieved,
for that was where our roots belonged, not in Harlow, where we
                                                        grieved.

I continued with my playing, I did solo turns in pubs,
at Weddings and Masonic Halls, and several different clubs.
I loved every single moment, for music was my life,
and many a gig I used to do, accompanied by my wife.
Alas, -- it all came to an end, one tragic awful day,
my fingers seemed to feel quite numb, and my hands, refused to
                                                            play.
It was diagnosed 'Neuritis,' it gave me quite a shock,
I landed up in hospital, for six weeks, I was in dock.
Unable to find a cure, I have suffered ever since,
to be parted from my music, still today, It makes me wince. ---

The Gift that God had given me, He thought best to take away,
for reasons only known to him, though still each day, I pray.
He replaced it with another gift, which gives me, enormous pleasure,
for I still write lots of poems, and this gift, --I'll always treasure.
I have three books to my credit, and I trust more on the way,
they were published not so long ago, and I'm writing one today.
To see them in the windows of the local shops in town,
it seems to lift my spirit, on those days that I feel down,
There's not much more on offer, in this world of trouble, and strife,
so I hope it's been of interest, 'This Story of my Life.'
I have now turned seventy four years old, and though you may think
me                                                    strange,
as I tell you with sincerity, that 'Not one day would I change.' ---

# WISH ME LUCK AS YOU WAVE ME GOODBYE

The platform was crowded with hundreds of troops,
some sat on their kitbags in small, little groups.
'Sweethearts, mothers, sad weeping wives,'
all cursing Hitler, for disrupting their lives!
The train at the platform, was packed like sardines,
with 'soldiers, sailors, airmen, marines!'
Some leaned from the windows, some stood at the door,
waiting to be whisked off, to fight Britain's War!

Behind smiles, and bravado, there lurked hidden fear!
which they tried not to show, as departure, drew near.
Porters hurried by with their trolleys, to and fro,
whilst troops still converged in continuous flow.
A distorted voice, from the speakers, blared out,
being difficult to distinguish, what it was all about!
Each compartment was full, not a seat going spare!
the corridor was stifling, with smoke, laden air!

To get to the toilet, people tripped over feet,
of the unlucky few who could not find a seat!
Fatigued, sweating bodies, occupied every space,
whilst latecomers frantically, searched for a place.
A few 'A.T.S. girls, and a couple of 'W.R.E.N.S,'
stood kissing goodbye to their sweethearts, and friends!
Smiles mingled with tears, was a most common sight,
with last minute instructions, 'Don't forget dear to write!'

On the soot laden forecourt of the station approach,
evacuee children were boarding a coach.
Their mothers looked on, with a stiff upper lip,
giving 'last minute cuddles, crying 'have a good trip!'
With their gasmasks and labels, which hung from their
                                                  neck,
they took to their seats for their long, unknown trek.
I had never experienced such a 'heart rending sight,'
as the poor, little buggers, prepared for their plight.
Several taxis pulled in, one after another!

trying their utmost to compete with each other.
On the platform, a porter shouted 'Please mind your backs!'
as he guided his truck, with 'G.P.O. mail-filled sacks!
A girl in stained overall, served 'hot cups of tea,'
to outstretching hands, which retrieved it with glee!
In and out the vast crowd, Military Police, they would
weave,
Checking the passes of soldiers on leave!
There was plenty got off from the incoming train,
those found without passes had a journey in vain!

As the minutes ticked by, it was soon time to go!
with kisses and hugs, the tears started to flow.
The Guard raised his green flag, and his shrill whistle blew,
with a hiss of steam and a shudder, the packed train
withdrew!
To not see them again, was the worst thing they feared,
as they waved their goodbyes, till the train disappeared.
It was hard to believe once again, we're at War!
the invasion of Poland, 'Well, it was the last straw!'
Could it possibly be true, that in this day and age,
that this terrible thing, could have got to this stage!
It had been a good summer, one of the best that we'd had,
and the scene that I'd witnessed, made me feel really sad!
It was only last year, they cried 'Peace in our time!'
Our unpreparedness for War 'was an unforgivable crime!'

# FAREWELL SWEET DREAMS

When I was a nipper those long years ago,
we came to a place which was called Walthamstow.
The house that we lived in, filled my mum with pride,
she was 'so overcome, that she broke down and cried.'
We were close to the shops, and the neighbours were nice,
after what we'd been used to, 'it was sheer paradise.' ---
Its spacious surroundings, to mum, was a boom,
and the afternoon sun, flooded into the room.
The bits that mum had, fitted just like a glove,
and the walls seemed to be, impregnated with love.
'Forty six Pembar,' I'll remember always,
for that's where I spent all my sweet childhood days.
Sweet are those memories that I still recall,
those years of my life, were the best of them all.

Each Sunday morning, I was up like a lark,
with a bagful of bread for the ducks at Lloyd Park.
From the old rustic bridge, I would throw in my bread,
as 'up waddled all the fat ducks to be fed.'
There was nothing quite like it on a hot summer's day,
than to sit in the park, and to hear the band play.
To watch the grey squirrels bound up the tall trees,
and the graceful white swans, that came gliding with ease.
Us kids on a Sunday, were always 'well clad,' ---
and we were a credit, to our mum and dad,
for that was the day that we wore our best clothes,
and we always looked smart from our head, to our toes.
Little girls proudly pushing their prams with their dolls,
and standing around watching tennis, and bowls.
A good game of cricket, was what I enjoyed most,
then 'home I would go, for my Sunday hot roast.'

The smell of roast beef, and greens, filled the air,
mum and dad after dinner, would doze in their chair.
With both their mouths open, they started to snore,
whilst the paper they shared, slithered down to the floor.

Quietly, I'd sit there, and not make a sound,
and patiently wait for tea-time to come round.
I can see them both now, as plain as could be,
as that picture still lives, in my sweet memory.

Mum did her week's washing on a Monday those days,
and under her copper, the fire would blaze,
It glowed like a jewel as it crackled, and spat,
spewing out small red embers, on the coconut mat.
It bubbled and gurgled, belching out scalding steam,
as the water ran down the damp walls in a stream.
The room smelt of soap, and was stiflingly hot,
as mum laboured away, till she'd finished the lot.
Washing days, my poor old mum used to dread,
as she dragged out the mangle, which stood in the shed.
'Clang, clang, went the cogs, as the rollers went round,'
as out gushed the water, which poured to the ground.
By the time mum was done, she looked really worn out,
and that was what washing day, was all about. ---

I will always remember those long afternoons,
the gold of the sun, in those lovely hot Junes.
Sometimes I went fishing down by the old stream,
with my rod in my hand, I would sit there and dream.
'Little white fluffy clouds streamed across the blue sky,
all the time I sat there, not a soul passed me by.
The big fish would sun themselves under the reeds,
and sometimes my line would get caught in the weeds.
On the slope of the bank neath the shade of a tree,
I would fish there for hours, in my sweet reverie.

The exchanging of comics, in those days was the trend,
with them under my arm, I'd pop round to my friend.
With my 'Wizard' and 'Hotspur' to add to my score,
I lifted the knocker and banged on the door.
'Come up,' bawled a voice, which took me unawares,
as I entered the cat smelling passage, and stairs.

'Have you read this?' and 'Have you read that?' ---
were the words we exchanged, as we sat on the mat.
With our business concluded, 'Off I would trot,'
feeling quite pleased, with the new ones I'd got.

The 'Pawn shops' in those days, they did a good trade,
in that era of hardship, with wages, low paid. ---
I was sent round to 'Pumphreys,' which was in Forest Road,
In time it became almost, 'my fixed abode.'
The man in the shop, got to know me quite well,
with my regular visits, which embarrassed me like hell.
I will always remember our mum's hard up days,
when into her poor empty purse, she would gaze.
Round to the pawn shop, twas me, she would send,
and 'what went in Monday, came out the weekend.'

I can picture mum now, sitting darning our socks,
with the open topped lid, of her needlework box.
With thimble on finger, and head bent down low,
backward and forward, the needle would go.
Her arthritic fingers, she worked to the bone,
not once did you hear my mum grumble, or groan.
She was placid by nature, and loved by us all,
and always responded to our beck, and call.
Without her, I don't know what we would have done,
for us, she did everything under the sun.

'How wonderful all those great days used to be,'
the thrill of a day trip, to Southend on Sea.
The fight that we had getting seats on the train,
'Oh how I wish for those days back again.'
Looking back on it now in the way that I do,
I would change not one day, of the life I once knew.
For sweet was the world in its own kind of way,
in spite of the hardship we saw every day.
Time seemed to stand still, and the days, they seemed long,
and as I look back now, I think, 'Where have they gone?' ---

# COLD MEAT 'N PICKLES

'Are you getting up or not?' shouted mum!
'I'm not gonna call you again!'
'If yer don't 'urry up, you'll be late for school,'
'and then you'll be getting the cane!'
With sleep in my eyes, and deep throated sighs,
I reluctantly crawled out of bed.
I slipped on my trousers, my socks and my shoes,
then pulled my shirt over my head.
I didn't like Mondays, they were always the same,
I hated the start of the week!
I drew back the curtain, peeped up at the sky,
and outside, the weather looked bleak.
A typical Monday! I said to myself,
I loathed them more than I can say!
I knew there'd be errands to run before school,
for Monday, was mum's washing day!

I came down to breakfast and what did I find?
the kitchen was clouded with steam!
I longed for the comfort of my cosy bed,
to be back in the land of my dream.
'You're down then?' said mum. 'About time, I must say,'
as she poured me a hot, cup of tea.
Then lifted a plate of hot toast from the hearth,
'Get stuck into that boy,' said she!
With sacking round waist, to and fro, my mum paced,
today, was her busiest day!
'Hurry up with your breakfast,' she'd holler to me,
'It's time it was all cleared away!'

With sleeves rolled up high, mum said with a sigh,
'I'll be glad when this blinkin lot's done!'
'I've so much to do, it' just isn't true,'
'and I want to be finished by one!'

With arms soaking wet, and her face bathed in sweat,
she plunged with the stick in the copper,
With the heat she recoiled, as it bubbled and boiled,
for the fire beneath, was a whopper!
Mum gave me the money to pop down the road,
there were one or two things she required,
she had been on the go since she got up at six,
no wonder poor mum looked so tired!
'You better get me some Persil,' cried mum,
'A large bar of soap, and some blue,'
'Take a cup for some pickle,' was my mother's cry,
'I can't stop, I've too much to do!'
I adored Stepney's pickles, I must say they were good,
the best I had tasted so far.
Oh that mouthwatering smell, as he dipped in the spoon,
and ladled them from the stone jar!
My favourite trick was to have a quick lick,
such temptation, I could not resist,
I dipped in my finger, its taste seemed to linger,
and I knew that it wouldn't be missed.

When I got back, mum was up to her neck,
sorting through shirts, sheets and smalls,
condensation played havoc in mum's small confined space,
and water  ran down the damp walls.
'You better be off then,' cried my dear old mum,
as the mangle was dragged through the yard.
I will never forget how fatigued, my mum looked,
Monday washdays, my goodness, were hard!
The washing she'd scrub, on the board in her tub,
her poor hands looked so red, and raw,
she wasn't done yet, and with feet soaking wet,
with the water all over the floor.

With the washing completed, it was hung on the line,
how mum managed it all, goodness knows,
she straightened her poor aching back with a sigh,
and her feet, and her fingers were froze.

My sister Win helped to gather them in,
mum's fingers, she'd worked to the bone,
the sheets and the shirts, they were all frozen stiff,
and dad's longjohns, stood up on their own!
Armfuls of clothes were brought in from the back,
they were draped round the fire to dry,
the room filled with vapour as they slowly thawed out,
mum complained how the time had flown by.
Each item was transferred to the clothes line above,
'Thank goodness for that! my mum said,
the trouble was each time one passed to and fro,
it compelled us to all duck our head.
Dad couldn't stand it dangling over above,
'Must you do this Nell?' dad used to growl,
'How else can I dry it?' my mum would reply,
and it always ended up in a row!

Though worn out and weary, mum still wasn't done,
'I'll be glad for my bed,' she would say,
'I've been on the go since the time I got up,'
and she'd iron them all the next day.
Life was hard years ago, there's no doubt about that,
the thirties was the Devil's Decade!
Labour saving devices were still yet to come,
what a difference now science has made!
When I think of mum now, through the sweat of her brow,
how she slaved for us all night and day,
she was One in a million, or should I say billion,
till the day that God took her away.

# MEMORIES OF WALTHAMSTOW

My memories always take me back to when I was a lad.
and as I wander through the years, it always makes me sad.
Oh God, how much I miss them! those 'happy days gone by,'
especially now I'm getting old, and know that soon, I'll die.
When I think of how life used to be 'Sixty, year ago,'
when our local market High Street was the 'Pride of Walthamstow!'
The humour of the Coster's as the crowds pressed round their stall,
although it was so long ago, 'those days, I still recall!'

All the old shops now have gone, I'm extremely sad to say,
I don't care what folk say to me, 'it's not the same today!'
there was, 'Cole and Deakins, Garnhams, Percivals, and Brands!'
'Barns and Harrods, Batemans,' 'all gone' or have changed hands!
'Liptons, Pearks and Maypole, Leslies, and Romains,'
'Lew Rose, Burtons, Davis's,' I remember all the names.
There was 'Walkers,' the dry cleaners, who did an excellent job,
they would 'clean and press your trousers, and only charged a bob!'
'Titas Ward and Lidstones,' to name but just a few,
every store have disappeared, and replaced by someone new!'
Now 'Fish Bros, Marks and Spencers,' are the recent ones to go,
'Who next?' I start to wonder, from our market, Walthamstow.

Most cinemas we knew and loved, have disappeared along the way,
I never thought in all my life, 'that I'd live, to see the day!'
The Palace too, has vanished, I think it was a sin,
to demolish such a building, for the shops no one go in!
The 'pride and joy of Walthamstow' of which it was renown,
even Hitler's bombers, couldn't knock the Palace down!

Along the busy Hoe Street, the trams they clanged their way,
the depot was in 'Chingford Road,' but no longer there today!
You didn't queue in those days, the people just jumped on,
and one did not have so long to wait, before one came along!
The conductors were a 'jolly' bunch, 'courteous' as well,
they helped you with your luggage, before they rang the bell!

Near the station in St. James Street, today I still recall,
was a cinema called 'The Regent' the 'worst one of them all!'
It wasn't very comfortable, and 'futile to complain,'
when it was difficult to hear the sound, through an 'approaching
train!'

It was regarded as 'the flea pit,' and referred to by that name,
they could not do much about it, I thought it was a shame!
It is now a Dental Practice, and busy, day by day,
But the memory of it lingers on, and with me, it will stay.

On the corner of Blackhorse Road, the 'Old Woolworths used to be,'
when I was a little lad, 'Oh how it intrigued me!'
Nothing over sixpence was their slogan in those days,
but in the early thirties, 'even that, was hard to raise!'
Easter was exciting, I was happy when it came,
you could buy an egg with violets on, and they'd even 'pipe your
name.'
Woolworth's Store was full of them, they had a good display,
contained inside, were chocolates, of Cadburys Best Milktray!
I looked forward to Good Friday, I loved my 'hot cross bun,'
and the Fair Bank Holiday Monday, where we had so much fun.
All those great times that I had, 'nostalgically, still flow,'
along with all my memories of 'Dear Old Walthamstow.'

# A FLEETING MEMORY

The thing that I loved most of all
back in my childhood days,
was a roaring fire on a winter's night,
I'll remember that always!
A great  big nob of shiny coal
would keep it in all night,
then mum would draw the curtains too,
and then, turn off the light.

sitting round the firelight glow,
to me, it was Sheer Bliss!
as I listened to the radio,
Oh, how those days I miss!
I loved to sit on top of it
till my knees were mottled red,
I would not budge a single inch,
till it was time for bed.

The comfort of a blazing fire,
still lingers in my mind,
it brightened up the dullest day
and a Blessing to mankind!
To come in from the bitter cold
it cheered one up no end,
and if you'd had a trying day,
a fire, was your friend.

There is nothing more congenial
than its warmth, and friendly glow,
it never failed to cheer you up,
if in spirit, you felt low!

It somehow helped you to unwind,
to relax and feel content.
your cares just seemed to drift away,
and it was heaven sent.
What we took for granted then,
we all miss so today,
the warm glow of a cheerful fire,
'What is there left to say?'


## THE PLIGHT OF THE PENSIONER

It seems so sad, that 'in this age,'
We have to 'suffer in silent rage!'
The indignity of 'being poor,'
Us folk, who helped to 'win the War!'

The 'pitiful pension we receive,'
'Perpetually, causes me to grieve.'
The 'cost of living, goes up each week,'
'Our future outlook,' 'Very bleak!' ----

It is hard to fathom, the 'reason why?'
We 'continually suffer,' until we die!
A 'substantial increase in our pay,'
Would alleviate our 'struggle, each day.'

'What others get,' you can't compare,'
And I think that it is 'so unfair!'
The 'small increase we get,' -- 'Oh Brother!'
'You give in one hand,' and 'take from the other.'

Our 'modest living,' has to suffice!
And, for 'holding our peace,' we're still, 'paying the price!'
The 'powers that be,' should be 'brought to heel,'
To 'give us poor Pensioners,' 'a far better deal!'
I have now reached the end of 'my little verse,'
And I wonder 'how long?' before things get 'much worse?'

# A PAUSE FOR THOUGHT

On my way to my sister, I have to pass my old school!
I'm usually in a hurry, and don't stop, as a rule!
For some unknown reason, on this day, I did,
It transported me back, to when I was a kid!

For a few fleeting moments, I paused in deep thought,
thinking of the Masters, and the subjects, they taught!
I could see myself entering that same, very, gate!
'Half scared to death! because 'I knew I was late!'

To this very day, in my mind, I recall,
Standing in rows, in the 'large, draughty hall.'
Beginning the day with the usual Lord's Prayer!
peeping through fingers, at the teacher's stern glare.

It was usually followed by a lecture from the Head!
And, 'Oh I wished I was still in my bed!
Any smiles from the teachers in those days, was sparse,
As to the sound of the piano, we were marched to our class!

One word from the teachers, and That was enough.
In those days, they were Strict, and was made of Stern Stuff.
It was more like a Prison, than it was like a School!
and they would not tolerate, 'Playing the Fool!'

Many a kid got a cuff round the head,
For not paying attention, to what teacher said.
In front of the blackboard, with his back to the class,
Figures appeared, which stood out, 'Bold as Brass!'

Determination to teach us, took not long, to discover,
as 'One hand held the chalk, and a cane in the other!'
Mathematical problems, were a difficult task,
as we sat there stewing, and too frightened to ask!

When the bell rang for playtime, it was a most welcome sound,
as we filed out in order, to the asphalt playground.
'Quick to punish, and slow to praise,'
That's what our schooling, was like in them days!

In the playground, a teacher would be on patrol!
and like a prison warder, kept us under control.
Ragged, arsed trousers, was our badge of the times,
Being so poor, was the worst of our crimes!

'Pale faces,' 'thin bodies,' was a common enough sight,
'Undernourishment, the culprit, to add to their plight,
Continuous scratching of the head, was a sure sign of fleas,
and some boys had festering, sores, on their knees!

I hated exams! for they made me feel ill!
My winning a Scholarship, was virtually nil!
I spent more time at home, than I did at my school,
I suppose that is why, I am such an old fool!'

I didn't realise the importance of a good education!
That is the reason for my present situation!
My passion for music, was too powerful to ignore!
Other subjects, they taught me, in comparison, was a bore!

I was not sorry when the time came to leave!
I was full of ambition, and yet so naive!
I left school at fourteen, in nineteen thirty eight,
not realising then, what I had on my plate.

I was soon disillusioned, my dreams became shattered!
A good education after all! Was what mattered!
I realised too late, I had been 'such a fool!'
The best years of your life, are when you are at school!

With a shrug of my shoulders, I went on my way,
Regretting my folly, until this very day.
My advice to you youngsters, is to 'learn all you can!'
Or you'll live to regret it, when you are an old man!

# THE SEASON OF GOODWILL

Christmas shopping today, I loathe,
because it costs so much, 'by jove.'
Each little thing you see's so dear,
I dread each day as it draws near.
With prices high, and pensions low,
'How quickly money seems to go?'
The yearly budgets, make me laugh,
'What do they do on our behalf?'
They give us ten pounds bonus, yes,
but each year it's worth less and less!
In the Common Market, we've missed the bus,
can you say 'What good, it's done for us?'

I feel sorry for the unemployed,
for the Christmases they once enjoyed.
Each year they see the prices rocket,
as they walk around with an empty pocket.
'How dispirited, they all must be?'
when they cannot buy the things they see!
The kids don't seem to understand,
why their dad's short tempered, and off hand.
They still expect expensive toys,
like all the other little boys!

'Oh wouldn't it be just a treat,'
to afford a nice big joint of meat?
A 'leg of pork,' a 'lump of beef,'
a 'sirloin steak,' to sink my teeth.
Wishful thinking! Yes I know,
but we could afford them years ago.
The Devil drives as and when needs must,
'Why is it that life's so unjust?'

The cost of food, the cost of drink,
is beyond our pocket, now, I think.
I ask you 'where is the good cheer?'
when it costs the earth for a pint of beer!
It's nothing like it used to be,
when Christmas meant so much to me!
It isn't worth the worry one bit,
I'm glad to see the back of it!
If this is the Season of 'Good Cheer,'
'Thank God it's only once a year!'

## THE SPIRIT OF THE LONDONER'S

With the 'blitz on London, at its height,'
'Bombs, raining down, each day, and night,'
The 'Londoner's, I still recall,'
'Faced up to it, and took it all!'
Of 'Demoralisation,' There was, 'no trace,'
With the 'horror, which they had to face!'
It's 'remarkable, that throughout each raid,'
The 'courageous courage,' 'which they displayed.;'

As 'fires raged,' and 'bombs rained down,'
It 'rekindled the spirit,' of 'London Town.'
The 'fire fighters, stood their place,'
'Still bore a grin, on blackened face.'
With the 'choking fumes,' that 'filled the air,'
They 'showed no sign,' of 'fear,' 'despair!'
A spaghetti of hoses, 'snaked the wet ground,'
'Complete devastation,' one could see, 'all around.'

'Bricks and mortar,' 'charred wood,' 'broken glass,'
Making it difficult for 'vehicles to pass!
'Tumbling buildings' 'falling walls,'
'Cries for 'assistance' -- 'distressing calls.'
'Bleeding hands, frantically, 'tearing through rubble,'
Only to find, 'a dead corpse,' for their trouble!'
Listening intently, for the 'sound of a voice,'

Effecting 'a rescue,' 'time to rejoice!'

'Reinforcements, requested to 'deal with the fires,'
A 'warehouse was burning,' 'chock-a-block, 'full of tyres.'
'More acrid smoke,' causing 'havoc to the lungs,'
A 'welcome mug of tea,' for 'dry thirsty tongues!'
Scorching heat from the fires, grew 'progressively worse,'
Intensive enough to 'melt coins in your purse!'
The 'red glow like the sunset,' seemed to blanket the sky,
With such 'raging inferno,' 'One could understand why.'

All one could see was 'huge buildings aflame,'
Whilst the 'drone of more aircraft 'which, - 'persistently came!'
Fingers of search-light , 'pierced the red sky,'
Many folk thought, 'they were going to die!'
Fresh fires started, as 'incendiaries rained down,'
Followed by a bomb, on the 'old Bull and Crown!'
As flames licked the woodwork, 'paint blistered and curled,'
Folk thought that it was, 'the end of the world!' ----

'How the Londoners took it,' 'Only God knows,'
Night after night, in 'damp shelters, they froze!'
Words fail to express, 'the sheer guts that they showed,'
'Defying the bombs' with a 'spirit that glowed!'
'They stayed put at home and they all did their bit,'
Thus 'proving to Hitler,' that the British had grit!'
'We can take it,' they cried!' overcoming their stress,'
As with 'shovels, and brooms,' they cleared up the mess.
'Fallen flakes, from the ceiling, 'soot,' 'broken glass!'
Swearing, 'if they saw Goering,' they would 'kick his fat arse!'
In the 'face of adversity,' 'one could not deny,'
That the 'backbone of Britain,' were folk, 'like you and I!'

With the 'bombing of London,' 'Adolf Hitler, was sure,'
Such 'devastation and horror,' would 'win him the War!'
Continuous bombardment, with 'daylight attacks,'
Failed to defeat, 'the most strongest of backs!'
Still to this day, 'they will 'live in my mind,'
this 'salt of the earth,' and 'the spirit of mankind!'

# PLACES I REMEMBER

There are places I remember, which still linger in my mind!
They rekindle tender memories of those days I've left behind.
Hemel Hempstead was my favourite, why I choose it is because,
it holds so many memories, I still see it as it was!
I was browsing through some photographs taken sixty years ago,
tears slowly trickled down my cheek, as my memories started to
flow.
We went there in the Forties, the second year of the War!
The raids were getting poor mum down, and she couldn't take no
more!
On the particular night in question, we had a very heavy raid.
I had never seen my darling mum so utterly, afraid.
The raids got more persistent, when the Blitz was at its height,
mum said, 'I'm off tomorrow! I can't stand another night!'

She scribbled a hasty note to dad, stating his dinner was on the stove,
mum, Win and I caught the 84 bus, from the Billet, to Arnos Grove!
We continued to St. Albans, via Barnet, and South Mimms!
When we got there, we were glad to stretch our stiff and aching
limbs.
The journey to Hemel Hempstead, was on a 'winding country lane!'
Past several little cottages, with fields of wheat and grain.
As the bus approached the Lime-Kilns, we alighted at a pub,
It was called 'The Leather Bottle' where we stopped to have some
grub.

We made our way to 'Apsley,' a little country town,
our cottage was in Orchard Street, a little further down.
Our host, was Mrs. Norris, a life long friend of mum.
Who welcomed her with open arms, and was pleased that she had
come.
Dad came down every Saturday, he was glad to get away.
He longed to get a good night's sleep, from the Raids each night and
day!
In the centre of the town, was a Pub called 'The Plough!'
We used to go there for a drink! 'It no longer is there now!

Opposite was a little stream, near the rose bed, on the green,
where the horses pulled in for their drink. Which was all part of the
scene.

Win missed her boyfriend Harold! much more than she could say.
Who promised her that very soon, that 'he would come down to
stay.
He was followed by his mum and dad, Mr. and Mrs. Lake.
And also his sister 'Maisie,' in her need to have a break!
We used to go for lovely walks, to explore the country lanes.
Strolling along, 'we'd sing a song! of those wartime, sweet refrains.
Hemel Hempstead was a pretty place, its beauty, I still recall!
Not far from it was 'Boxmoor,' which was loved by one and all.
St. Johns Road was so picturesque! Graced with 'Poplar, Oak and
Beech!'
and the ever popular 'Grand Union Canal' was quite within our
reach.
We paused to watch the 'sturdy horse,' tow the gaily painted barge,
Its muscular body which bore the strain, led by the man in charge.
Not every barge which plied the canal, possessed an engine, or a
funnel!
The bargee lying on his back, 'had to leg it through the tunnel!'

The town possessed two cinemas,' 'The Luxor, and Princess!'
The entrance fee was ninepence! or sometimes, even less!
It was affordable in those days, it was our mid-week treat,
At the corner of 'Two Waters!' that was where we used to meet.
We waited for the first bus, to take us into town.
It only cost a penny, from the bus stop further down.

Mr Norris was a dear old soul, and a 'proper country yokel!'
With his wife Ada, arm in arm, they'd stroll to 'The Spotted Dog!'
their local!
Whilst sitting in his favourite chair, and eating his apple tart,
he sometimes, lifted the cheek of his arse, and eject a 'triple fart!'
His face expressed his sheer relief, by the expression he had on it!
And for a while, wreathed a smile, saying, 'That was a good'n wan't
it?'

I used to feel embarrassed, but got used to it in time,
he said 'To bottle up the wind, 'was a silly useless crime!'

From all those long, long years ago, my mind recalls it still!
There was 'Win and Harold,' 'mum and dad,' 'Harold's sister Maise,
Bill!'
It was very soon I got to know of all the pubs in town,
The 'Six Bells,' was my favourite, and it was so well renown!
It was five minutes walk from Featherbed Lane, where for walks, we
used to go!
All singing as we made our way, down that lane that we loved so.
We congregated in the lounge, nearly every Sunday morn!
where we stuffed ourselves with sandwiches, of 'pickle, cheese, or
brawn!'
When Harold's mum and dad popped in, it was usually after one!
They'd be just about exhausted, from the long walk they had done.

Whatever pub I went to, my 'Accordion!' it came too,
it was part and parcel of my life, of those days that I once knew!
The landlady Vi, would smile and say, 'well what about a tune?'
I was only too happy to oblige, and at the same time, over the moon!
It meant money in my pocket, which I'd never had before,
for they always had a whip round, before I came out the door.
Usually the place got packed, not an inch of room to spare,
They sang along with every song, all the Londoners that were there.

Fresh watercress flourished in the clear, swift flowing stream.
They sold it for one penny, and its taste, it was supreme.
Dad often bought a pen'orth, for our Sunday evening tea,
We had it with shrimps, or winkles, which were all fresh from the
sea.

My years of Hemel Hempstead, were the best I've ever had.
Whenever I think of Hemel now, I can see my mum and dad!
It was many, many years later, when I went back there again,
To renew my pleasant memories, with a walk along Lawn Lane.
When my bus got to St. Albans, I stopped for a quick snack,
Before resuming on my journey, where I so longed to be back.

That pleasant country ride I knew, I am grieved to have to say,
Had changed from a beautiful country lane to a 'busy motor-way!'
When I got to Hemel Hempstead, I walked towards the town,
The many changes that I saw, made me really feel so down!

Gone was that little pub, 'The Plough!' with its welcome on the mat,
Where the locals got together, for their friendly drink, and chat.
That pretty little stream had gone, where the horses had their drink.
It was now a dried up, piece of ground, but for 'Why I just can't
think!'

The quaint little shops that I knew, and loved, had all but
disappeared.
Superstores had taken their place, with the changes I had feared.
I went into the 'Six Bells Pub,' for a drink, for 'old times sake!'
Where I immediately thought of mum and dad, and of Mr. and Mrs.
Lake!
Sitting there, I could not believe, it was all those years ago!
As I supped my beer, there came a tear, as I let my memories flow.
I could picture us just like we were, all young and in our prime!
singing all those wartime songs, which were so popular at that time.
I felt sadness creep into my heart, and felt lonely, as could be!
But before I made my way back home, I had one more thing to see.

I made my way to the Watercress bed, and to my horror, and dismay,
I found a 'Cesspit full of garbage!' T'was the last stroke!, Come What
May!
I just could not believe my eyes, as they took in what they saw,
This was not the Hemel Hempstead, that I knew all through the War!
If that is what's called 'Progress,' then I'll eat my blessed, hat!
But I still have my sweet memories, 'Thank Goodness God, for
That!'
I must say I was very glad to get back on the bus!
My ultimate conclusion was 'more minus's, than plus's!
I felt so disillusioned, it's myself I have to blame!
For imagining Hemel Hempstead, would today, still look the same!
This poem I have written, gives me pleasure to impart!
along with all those memories, which are embedded in my heart.

# A TRIBUTE TO MY DARLING MOTHER

My darling Mum, she passed away at eighty seven years old,
and in her loving body, beat a heart of pure gold.
I can visualise her dear face now, watching over us with care,
I can't tell you how it hurts me, when I see her vacant chair.
Everybody loved my mum, 'so placid, sweet and kind,'
she left us all with 'broken hearts,' when she left this world behind.

When we were kids, our aches and pains, she soothed with words of
love,
and now she's with the angels, in God's Heaven up above.
Quite often I still think of her, when I'm sitting all alone,
this 'angel of love,' who always worked her fingers to the bone.
The hardship that she suffered in life, 'no one will ever know,'
'Oh how we miss her dear sweet face,' and the love that she bestow.

She slaved for us when we were kids, in her struggle to keep us fed,
'Oh the worried look upon her face,' and the tears she often shed.'
When we came home to dinner from school, as hungry as the day,
our plates were full, 'except my mum's,' 'I'm not hungry,' she would
say.
So many times unbeknown to us, she must have gone without,
'back in the hungry thirties,' that's what life was all about. ---

Perennial poverty seemed to rear its ugly head each day,
the hours were long, the work was hard, low was the average pay.
How mum managed, 'I'll never know,' but somehow she pulled
through,
she always kept us kids well fed, and my dear father too.
Dad never earned a lot them days, and life was one long struggle,
every penny that my parents had, they always had to juggle.
As I look back to the times and life, of the world I used to know,
I always think of Mum and Dad, as each memory starts to flow.
'Oh how I wish they were with me now,' more than my heart can say,
especially my ole darling mum, who I think of each day.

I thought the world of my dear Mum, no one could take her place,
'Oh golly what I wouldn't give,' just to kiss her dear sweet face.
My thoughts are with her always, till this world I do depart,
her beloved memory will always dwell, deeply in my heart.

# GOOD INTENTIONS

If I could win some money,
'Oh the Good, that I would do.'
I would help the 'Poor, and needy,'
and Of Course, 'My Family, too.'
I would give a lot to 'Charity',
where I thought would do Most Good,
If Only, it would Come my way,
I swear to you, 'I Would.'

This isn't Just mere, Idle talk,
I mean every word I say,
for 'nothing in life, would 'please me more!'
than 'giving Some away,
What Good, would money Do me now?
if I may be so bold,
I would never live to Spend it all,
at 'Seventy three, years old.

I would give to 'Animal Sanctuary's'
for the 'Good Work that they do,'
The 'Home for Retired, horses,'
and the P.D.S.A. too.'
Every week, I do the Lottery,
but Nothing, Comes my way,
I only do a 'Pound's worth,'
and to 'Win, Would Make My Day,'
I often get 'two numbers up,'
but Somehow 'Never Three,'
Oh dear, it's so frustrating,'
I'm sure, you Would agree,
Money, always goes to money,
Isn't 'it a Sin?'
for' 'Those who would do 'Good, with it,'
'They 'Never, get a Win.'

## FALSE ALARM

On everyone's lips, was the talk of a War,
and 'Be prepared leaflets,' were pushed through our door.
Round every street, came the 'Loud Speaker Van,'
stating 'Please get your gasmasks, as soon as you can.'
The prospect of peace, became 'thinner, and thinner,'
that announcement put me, and my mum, off our dinner.

'Come on,' Dad said, 'We must go round the school,'
and when we arrived there, the place, it was full.
Outside the door, stood a long waiting queue,
and it took quite a time, before we all got through.
To get us all fitted, twas no easy task,
as each person there, tried on mask after mask.

They were issued to us, in a small cardboard box,
and were kept on our sideboard, with the vases and clocks.
Every so often, our mask, we would don,
to see what it felt like, when we kept them on. ---
The smell of the rubber, 'it made me feel sick,'
and the noise they emitted, used to get on my wick.
Your breath left a residue, of moisture inside,
and the visor went misty, which I could not abide.
I felt suffocated, and started to cough,
and only too glad, when I took the thing off.
'You've got to get used to it,' Dad he would say,
but Mum said, 'For Christ sake,' let's put them away.'

'Anderson Shelter's' became common sight,
Dad furnished ours out, with some chairs, and a light.
They were sunk in the gardens, 'three feet, below ground,'
with construction completed, 'they were quite firm and sound.'
Strong nuts and bolts, held them firmly together,
the only snag then was, 'the damp, rainy, weather.'
The bottom got flooded, whenever it rained,
and every so often, it had to be drained.
Their entrance was small, to climb in, and get out,
especially for those folk, who were a bit stout.

It happened at times, a fat person got stuck,
it was a tight squeeze, and ;they didn't arf ruck.'
Earth was banked up, round the sides and the top,
'What a good job he made of it,' my dear old pop. ---

Trenches were hastily dug in the parks,
everybody mucked in, 'Council workers,' and 'Clerks.'
'Sandbags were hastily filled by the score,'
stacked in front of the buildings, and each side of the door.
'Volunteers were enlisted, for the 'Civil Defence,'
whilst bated breaths waited, for the War to commence.
We were taught what to do in the event of a raid,
how to deal with incendiaries, and 'administer first aid.'
Searchlights beamed fingers, in the dark of the night,
and precautions were taken, to block out the light.

I shall always remember 'Nineteen thirty eight,'
when Britain had more than her share on her plate.
We all felt relief from that burden we bore,
when Chamberlain dragged peace, from the jaws of a War.
The main trouble was, that we were not prepared,
and did not stand a chance, had a War been declared.
During that crisis, the people kept calm,
and avoiding the War, gave us chance to re-arm.
Mr. Chamberlain said, 'It was Peace in our time,'
but he proved to be wrong, in 'Nineteen thirty nine.'
I can still see him now, as he stepped from that plane,
waving that paper, again and again.
When he read out its contents, they started to cheer,
with relief on their faces, which had shown so much fear.
As I end this story, those memories still cling,
of that piece of paper, which was not worth a thing.
A Second World War, they tried hard to deter,
'It just goes to show you, 'How wrong they all were.' ---

## BETWEEN THE WARS

In the twenties and thirties when history was made,
it was sometimes referred to, as 'the Devil's Decade.'
In those days I was just a ragged arsed lad,
who got more clouts than ha'pennies, from my dear old dad.
Times they were hard, and the people were poor,
and many a hawker came round the street door.
My soft hearted mother, bought stuff every day,
for she hadn't the heart, to turn them away.
Though she could not afford it, mum bought their old tack,
'no wonder the buggers, they kept coming back.'

To have stuff on tick in those days was the trend,
we paid for it Friday, or at the weekend.
Our bill used to come to about fifteen bob,
and to meet it at times, was a bit of a job.
The pawn shops round our way, they did a good trade,
humiliation, was the price that we paid.
There was always a queue standing outside the door,
'Oh what a curse,' it was to be poor. ---

Sometimes on a Sunday, we went up the lane,
we would walk to St James Street, and jump on the train.
It was crowded with people as we pushed our way through,
all hunting for bargains, like they used to do.
From end to end, stood the rickety stalls,
and secondhand clothing hung up on the walls.
I loved going up there, it made a nice break,
we did so much walking, my legs used to ache.
When we came home, our bags, they were full,
with second hand clothing, which I wore for school.

The old High Street market, I used to adore,
on Saturday nights, there were bargains galore.
I often went up there with my dear old mum,
and from miles away, the people would come.
I will always remember those green naphtha lights,
that hissed on the stalls on those Saturday nights.

There was something about them that's hard to explain,
but they live in my memory, again and again.
The stallholder's humour, still lives in my mind,
from those wonderful days which we've now left behind.
Those colourful characters of long long ago,
were the backbone of High Street, of old Walthamstow.
The Carlton, and Palace, we looked on with pride,
there was always a long queue of people outside,
entertainment was good, and cheap at the price,
and if we could afford it, we did not think twice.

The old Co-op Divi, was a bob in the pound,
it helped my old mum make her money go round.
It may not sound much in these days it is true,
but it was quite a lot in nineteen thirty two.
I recall still the fragrance of freshly baked bread,
for a nice crusty loaf, twas a lot to be said,
down the road every day, came the old baker's cart,
his hot bread and cakes, won their way to my heart.
The traders those days used to come round the door,
the 'Butcher,' the 'Grocer,' and quite a few more.
They were glad of your custom, they valued it dear,
and they gave you a Christmas box, once every year.

How life has changed since I was just a boy,
when the small things in life, seemed to fill us with joy.
Christmas those days, to us, meant a lot,
we were grateful for all the small gifts that we got.
Unlike today, the true meaning, was there,
the Christmases now, you just cannot compare.
People gave parties, and their friends came along,
they stood round the piano, and each gave a song.
Thank heaven that there were no telly's them days,
but live entertainment, which was all the craze.
In spite of the poverty, struggle, and strife,
I must say they were, the best days of my life.

# A BLESSED COMPANION

I adore my 'local library,' it's a Godsend I must say.
for 'Books, are my salvation,' I read them every day.
I appreciate 'good literature,' an 'author that's renown,'
if I find a book which appeals to me, 'I cannot put it down.'

Like a 'soft and soothing melody,' it brings 'solace to my soul,'
to discover a book which I think I'll like, then I'm 'half way to my
goal!'
I'm a 'very avid reader,' spending many hours each day,
Relaxing with a 'favourite book,' if 'by chance, one comes my way.'

Like a 'sponge absorbing water,' it is difficult to hide,
my 'thirst for a good story,' 'I am never satisfied!'
When I discover a 'good author,' 'I stick to them like glue,'
'Catherine Cookson,' 'Josephine Cox,' and numerous others too.

They have 'won my admiration,' for the 'brilliance of their work!'
and, 'in my local library,' is where, 'usually I lurk.'
if I haven't got a book to read, 'it fills me with despair,'
like a 'fish that's out of water,' which is 'gasping for its air!'

I 'cannot emphasise, enough,' how important to me this is,'
To have a decent book to read, 'to me, it is sheer bliss!'
'On occasions, I've been forced to leave, without a single book,'
When I've found that I've read most of them, 'it is futile then to
look!"

The 'more I read, the more I need,' 'it's as simple folks as that!'
The day I give up reading, 'is the day, I'll eat my hat!'
I cannot choose at random, the type of book, I need,

It isn't easy to always find, the 'books, I like to read.'

The books in my possession, I treat with 'utmost care!'
'Unnecessary damage,' I simply cannot bear!'
There's 'nothing which annoys me more,' than to 'see a dog-eared
page,'
There is 'no excuse for such abuse,' in this 'normal day and age.'

If only people realised, 'how expensive, they've become,'
I'm 'sure that they would 'think again' before they used their thumb!'
It matters 'not who reads them! a dustman, or a duke,'
It's the 'way they are mishandled, that 'makes me want to puke.'

I 'wallow in nostalgia,' I 'relish it with joy!'
Nostalgia brings forth memories, of 'when I was a boy.'
Stories about 'sweet childhood days,' 'I can never get enough,'
Though 'some folk often say to me, 'how can you like that stuff?'
They say, 'I should look forward,' 'instead of looking back,'
When I tell them 'I prefer to,' 'I get a lot of flack!'

Each of us, 'have different tastes,' 'We can't all think the same,'
I 'know the stories that I like,' so 'I don't care what they claim.'
I'm sad to say, 'this world today,' leaves a lot to be desired,'
That is 'why I give my thanks to God, for those memories, I've
acquired.'

I have reached the 'twilight of my life,' 'I am seventy four years old!'
And my 'best companion, 'is a book,' to me it's pure gold.'
You can 'keep your televisions,' 'I can't be bothered to look!'
Just give me a 'cosy corner,' an 'armchair,' and a 'book.'
I do not ask a lot from life, I am 'easily contented!'
To me, a book's the most 'precious thing,' 'that's ever been invented!'

# THE MIRACLE OF DELIVERANCE

My dear brother Reg, was at Dunkirk.
Where our lads, had their backs to the sea.
The stukers streaked down and 'dive bombed them,'
When our brave lads were trying to flee.
The 'carnage, destruction, around them,'
Was a sight they will never forget,
It will 'live in their poor minds forever,'
As 'gradually in closed the net!'
Encircled by 'powerful forces,'
They did not know 'which way to turn?'
And hearing the news on the wireless,
Caused their loved ones at home, 'Great concern.'

'Thousands of craft of all sizes,'
Met up, as they 'put out to sea,'
To 'bring back our boys, that were stranded,'
Who fought ;'bravely, to keep us all free.'
Ploughing on, in their 'errand of mercy,'
They battled their way through the foam,
Disregarding their 'own personal safety,'
To 'bring all our boys, safely home!'

Under 'constant attack on the beaches,'
Our brave boys put up a 'good show.'
Determined 'not to surrender,'
Hitting back, where they could, at the foe!'
Digging in, best they could, under pressure,
'Dive-bombed, and straffed from the air.'
Preparing themselves, for departure,
With 'hope in their hearts and a prayer.'

As they 'struggled in their bid, for survival,'
Some ships, got 'blown out of the sea,'
In their 'undying effort to make their escape,'
To fight on in 'The land of the free!'

In their 'undaunting 'courage and valour,'
With 'their comrades, who fought by their side,'
Helping the wounded, to get to the boats,
with a 'prayer for their mates, who had died.'

Still under constant bombardment,
They waded, chest high through the sea.
Ready to board any vessel,
Which they scanned the horizon to see.
Those 'Veterans,' who are no longer with us,
'In our hearts, in our minds, they still lurk,'
For 'never' will they 'ever be forgotten,'
Or the 'miracle of their deliverance from Dunkirk.'

# A BLAST FROM THE PAST

My Mum and Dad were moving, they'd got a 'Warner's Flat,'
everything was ready to go, bar the lino, and the mat.
Mum said, 'I'll take them with me,' 'Why should I leave them
behind?'
'You can bung them in the passage, with the curtains, and the blind.'
I helped my Dad to roll it up, while mum looked for some twine,
'Underneath it, there were papers, dated 'nineteen thirty nine.'
The Headline stated 'PEACE, OR WAR? WE SHALL KNOW AT
NOON TODAY.'
It took my mind back 'thirty years,' as my thoughts began to stray.
I squatted on a tea-chest, with the paper on my knee,
whilst Mum went in the other room, to make a cup of tea.
'That's an old un, 'Ain't it boy?' my Father turned and said,
'That brings back some memories Den,' - as 'every bit I read.'

Old memories they came flooding back, like they'd never done
before.
I could see us round the wireless, hearing 'Britain Was At War.'
It was followed by the warning, which frightened my poor Mum,
which caused her knees to tremble, with butterflies in her tum.
Dad told her 'not to worry,' just to 'sit there and keep calm,'
and the warning as happened, 'proved to be a false alarm.'
The nest day, my poor Mum was off, 'she stayed with 'Len and
Rose,'
at their country house at Baldock, 'that's the place where Mother
chose.'
She made her way to Finsbury Park, to catch the morning train,
'It took several weeks of the phoney war, 'till my Mum came home
again.'

My Dad was in the A.R.P,' like many many, more.
he felt he'd like to do his bit, to help to win the war.
I can see him in his tin hat now, with his 'Whistle,' and his Torch,'
filling buckets with sand and water, that was kept in our front porch.
I could visualise the way it was, as the bombs came whistling down,
and the way old Jerry used to clobber, 'Poor old London Town.'

The endless queues outside the shops, the shortages of food,
as I sat there reminiscing, in my sweet, nostalgic mood.
I remembered all those 'meatless days,' the notorious 'Woolton Pie.'
The weekly packet of 'powdered egg,' which my Mother used to buy.
'Gone were those days of luxury, when we had 'eggs and ham,'
and in their place 'what did we get?' 'sausages,' and 'spam.' --
The little food we used to get, 'wasn't enough to feed a cat,'
with the 'losses to our shipping,' 'we were lucky to get that.'

As I wandered through those darkened years, and what we all went
                                                        through,
the 'sleepless nights,' the 'blackout,' all seemed 'too much to be true.'
I suppose we're very lucky now, to think we're still alive.'
there's not many of us left today, who were 'fortunate to survive.'
I thought of those poor little kids, 'the large scale evacuation,'
being whisked away from their dear Mums, to some unknown
                                                        destination.
The 'Doodlebugs,' the 'rockets,' the 'destruction from the air,'
the 'uncertainty,' and 'misery,' that we all had to bear.
The 'heartbreak,' and the 'sorrow,' the 'sacrifice,' and 'tears,'
The 'fear,' that everybody shared, through 'six long struggling years.'

Came my rude awakening, with a 'knock upon the door,'
as 'In stomped two removal men, 'dragging tea-chests from the floor.'
My 'daydreams' they were over, it was time for us to go,
'It's funny how a 'paper' can make 'all those memories flow.'
We hopped into the waiting van, which struggled with its load,
as it made its way to Mum's new flat, which was in 'Badlis Road.'
'How quickly all those years have gone, 'they seem to go so fast,'
'All that's left of them are memories,' that 'sweet blast from the past.'

## PARADISE

Heaven has its angels,
somewhere up there, is mum!
She's earned her place in Heaven,
God wanted her to come!
When the sun is shining,
she is smiling down on me,
from her new home up in Heaven,
where she dwells in ecstasy.

Whenever there's a rainbow,
high up in the sky,
it's the aura which surrounds her,
where spirits never die.
When it rains it's merely tears of joy,
from the angels up above,
because they're re-united,
with the ones they really love.

Jesus said 'There is no death,
if you believe in me,'
'Everlasting life awaits you,'
'That's my promise unto thee!'
'When your life on earth has been fulfilled,'
'I'll prepare a place for you,'
'Hand in hand, we'll walk together,'
'When you bid your life adieu!'

If I were an artist,
a picture I would paint,
of Mum's new home in Heaven,
because she was a Saint!
Although she had a hard life here,
she now has her reward,
in everlasting beauty,
in the home of our dear Lord.

She deserved her place in Paradise,
for what my mum went through,
till the gates of Heaven beckoned her,
to start her life anew.
Though it broke her heart to leave us,
which was more than she could bear,
they welcomed her with open arms,
into their loving care.

Her Spirit is still with us,
every hour of the day,
and in the stillness of the night,
I think of her, and pray!
'God bless you, dearest, darling Mum,'
'Until we meet again,'
'Continue smiling down on me,'
'From our dear Lord's Domain!'

# HOW LIFE USED TO BE

As I look back to the past on how life used to be,
all those memories long ago, come flooding back to me.
My childhood days, I used to love, more than my heart can say,
life was so very different then, to how it is today.
Sweet was that world I used to know, when I was still a boy,
I found it was the simple things that filled me so with joy.
Every day to me, seemed long, and time was on my side,
although we had our ups and downs, we took them in our stride.

I often sit and think of all the good times that we had,
and when I do, I must confess, 'I can't help feeling sad.'
They call the thirties bad old days, 'to me, each one was gold,'
it seems like only yesterday, as memories, they unfold.
So many things have disappeared, that made our life worth while,
that act of common courtesy, and service with a smile.
Good manners and politeness, to name but just a few,
that little thought for others, in that world that I once knew.
Time can't erase those memories that still linger in my heart,
to describe the changes that I've seen, 'I don't know where to start.'
Change and decay, I'm sad to say, in all around I see,
gone have the good things in this life, that meant so much to me.

Gone have the little corner shops of my sweet childhood days,
'the friendly grocer that we knew,' which once was all the craze.
'The rattle of the milk cart,' the 'clanging of the tram,'
'The penn'orth of mustard pickles, and the 'ha'pennyworth of jam.'
'The Variety Theatres,' where I always loved to go,
especially the 'Old Palace,; of our High Street Walthamstow.
'The tuppenny and the penn'orth, which tasted so divine,
'the few bob in my pocket,' which I happily called mine. ---
'Blessed were the hungry,' the 'sick,' the 'lame,' the 'poor,'
'Blessed were the 'hawkers,' who went from door to door.'
'Blessed my dear mother,' and those words she used to say,
'I feel so sorry for them,' 'How could I turn them away?' ---
She always bought a thing or two, 'no matter then how small,'
though 'hard up,' was my mum herself, those days that I recall.

Gone have the 'Pearly Kings and Queens,' we don't see them today,
who did lots of work for charity, in their kind and humble way.
Gone has our 'Mighty Empire,' which filled our hearts with pride,
and those 'cheap day excursions,' which whisked us to the seaside.
Gone has the 'lovely music,' and the 'songs we used to sing,'
and 'that field adjacent to my school,' where we played 'kiss in the
ring.'
Those 'little girls,' with golden curls, whom I used to chaperone,
they are 'all grown up and married,' and have families of their own
'How quickly all those years have flown,' since my 'sweet childhood
days,'
when all those little games we played, were just a passing phase.
Here I am at seventy four, still dwelling in the past,
'It was such fun,' when I was young, 'what a shame it doesn't last?'

# BRICK LANE

'How much do yer want for 'em?' my father cried.
as he looked for the faults which the man tried to hide.
He was buying some secondhand clothes for my Win
for the winter had come, and her frocks were so thin.
He picked up some boots, which you laced with a hook,
and his trained eye missed nothing, as he had a good look,
'That's a good bit 'O leather,' said the man on the stall,
'She'll be glad of 'em mate, when the snow starts to fall.'
Dad's critical eye spotted one or two flaws,
that he showed to the man who was wearing plus-fours.
'Well yer don't 'ave ter 'ave 'em ole gov,' said the man,
'You find 'em cheaper somewhere else if you can.'
'Well how much yer asking?' said dad with a frown,
the man picked them up and said, 'gi's 'alf a crown.'
'Two and a tanner,'-- said my dad in disgust,
'With customers like you,' said the man, 'I'd go bust.'

'I'll 'ave 'em,' said dad, 'if you make it two bob,'
'she can't wear 'em like this, it's a job for the snob.'
The stallholder paused with the boots in his hand,
as their soles, and their uppers, his beady eyes scanned.
'I'm losing money on these,' snarled plus-fours,
'Okay, two bob, and the boots, they are yours.'
Dad fished in his pocket, and pulled out the cash,
dropped the boots in his bag, with the rest of the trash.

He picked up a skirt, which he thought would fit Win,
his other hand stroking his rough, whiskered chin.
He inspected it closely, as if in deep thought,
not once had my father yet ever been caught.
He laid it aside, and continued to browse,
from the junk on the stall, he extracted a blouse.
'How much you asking for these then,' croaked Dad,
'and what do yer want for this cap for the lad?'
The next thing I knew, it was plonked on my head,
'Let's see if it fits yer?' my dear father said.

To my great delight, the cap fitted a treat,
it went with my coat which came down to my feet.
Its previous owner's name was inside,
on a piece of white tape, about half an inch wide.
In Capital Letters, it spelt out 'John Smith,'
and just below that, there was scrawled 'Upper fifth.'
The man on the stall said 'three bob for the lot,'
and dad seemed quite pleased with the stuff that he'd got.

Dad then sorted out a 'V neck woollen dress,
'One and six,' said the man, 'and not one penny less.'
'Can you make it a shilling?' said dad with a sigh,
'Not on your life mate,' came the stallholder's cry.
'You've already done me for quite a few bob,'
and under his breath, dad said 'bloody good job.'
Dad paid him the money and off we both went,
whilst dad reckoned up how much money he'd spent.
As we wandered away, I carried the bag,
'Hold it,' screamed dad, 'while I roll me a fag.'

The next thing dad bought, was 'cups, saucers and plates,'
from a stall further on, stacked with open topped crates.
'Just what mum can do with,' said dad with a smile,
'Let's hope they last her for quite a long while.'
Each piece was emblazoned with some sort of crest,
Dad said that my mother must keep them for best.
'As used by the Gentry,' cried the bald headed man,
'Don't stand there gawping, snap 'em up while yer can,'
'Only a tanner a piece do I ask,'
and in between breaths, swigged some tea from his flask.
Dad bought what he wanted, and was pleased as could be,
he then bought some winkles to take home for our tea.
He called in at the pub to have a quick dram,
then out my dad came, and we boarded the tram.

Dad gave me a wink as we groaned on our way.
I was pleased with my cap, it had been a good day.
I felt starving hungry, and longed for my dinner,
mum's roast beef, and yorkshire, was always a winner.
Sister Win, she was pleased with her secondhand clothes.
They all seemed to fit her, though how, goodness knows.
As for dad, he was pleased, 'cause he'd saved a few bob,
and my mum liked the China, and she said, 'just the job.'
Now I must say that dad was a very shrewd man.
he was more like his father, but not like my gran.
My father told me it's not so daft as it sounds,
for if I saved my pennies, they would turn into pounds.
Dad always was careful where cash was concerned,
and saved a few bob form the wages he earned.
He has always been thrifty as far as I know,
saying from little acorns, great oak trees, they grow.
He informed me that next time he goes up the lane,
if I saved my fare, he would take me again.

# GONE BUT NOT FORGOTTEN

I sat down on my usual seat, outside of Woolworth's Store.
I was glad to rest my aching feet, because they felt so sore.
With my heavy bag of shopping, I felt just about 'all in!'
and I had to keep my eyes peeled, to catch my sister Win.
I watched the busy shoppers as they ambled to and fro,
the traffic from the Palmerston, was one continual flow.

There was a dear old lady who was sitting next to me,
who said 'This High Street's not the same, like how it used to be!'
I agreed with her wholeheartedly, for I knew that she was right,
it was nothing in comparison, of a Pre-War, Saturday night.
It sparked off happy memories, of which I still recall,
I could smell the fumes from the naptha lights,
as they hissed on every stall.
The Coster's were so cheerful, each had a smiling face!
They laughed, and joked, with everyone, it was a happy place!
The atmosphere was different then, to what it is today,
their fruit and veg, was cheap to buy, which they almost gave away.

There were no queues in those days, it was 'first come, first served.'
I still hold them in high esteme, a reward, that they deserved!
Saturdays were a joy to me. The market blazed with light,
the shops and stalls, were thriving till, gone ten o'clock at night.
It was left to the last minute, when people bought their joint,
it saved them quite a bit of cash, so you can see their point.
It was auctioned off quite cheaply, that bit extra on the top,
a bit of tripe, or sausages, or perhaps a lean pork chop!
Rockbottom prices drew the crowd, the sale was at its peak,
up would shoot their eager hands, for the bargain of the week.

My mum would pop into the Cock, for her half a pint of stout,
whilst I popped into Manz's for a jolly good blow out.
The Fish shops did a roaring trade, especially Saturday night,
folk strolling along eating fish and chipps, was quite a common
                                                    sight.
It was either that, or Saveloys, with piping hot pease pudd,
the German buthcers were the best, for the taste was really good.

101

There were lots of entertainment, Cinema's galore,
and outside the Walthamstow Palace, people queued up at the door.
For just a matter of coppers, one could have a good night out,
it transported you to a different world, that's what life was all about!

Every Saturday regular, the Sally army band,
congregated on the corner, and they sounded really grand.
I often stopped to listen with upliftment in my heartl,
resplendent in their uniforms, they really looked quite smart!
A handful of Ex Servicemen made Saturday nights complete,
rattling their boxes, as they shuffled down the street.
One could not help but sympathise the misfortune of their plight,
in their tattered, braided uniform, they looked a sorry sight.

Allowing my mind to wonder, I'm transported back in time.
The world was a much nicer placer, there wasn't so much crime.
I would not wish myself young again, the way things are today,
for I lived in much better times, I'm very pleased to say!
There is so much to look back on. Fortunately, I can,
to have lived in that great era, 'I'm a very lucky man!'

# PROGRESS

No matter What you Buy today, 'It isn't meant to last!'
'Reliability,' Sad to say, is 'Something of the Past.'
Let's take for instance, 'Cooker's, 'Washing Machines, and Dryers,'
'Cordless kettles,' 'Irons,' and perhaps, 'Electric Fires.'
'Recorder's, 'Televisions,' 'Whatever you Care to mention,'
it 'Isn't long, till they go Wrong, and Soon, require attention.'

Look at all the Cars, today, 'Just a tap, and there's a Dent,'
and 'Look how much it Costs you,' 'Almost every, Cent!'
Today, things are 'Inferior,' to What they used to be,
years ago, 'They were Made to Last,' and the 'Pride of Industry.'

Central Heating, is another thing! 'Just Look What Can Go Wrong!'
Once the Boiler Starts to wear, then, 'It's the Same Old Song.'
'It's difficult to get the Parts,' is What they Usually say,'
"This particular model is Out of Date,' and 'This has had its Day.'
'For what it'll cost you for Repair,' 'You might as well 'Buy New!'
Oh Yes, 'We've heard it All Before,' and We don't know What to
Do!'

As soon as you have trouble, you Call an Engineer,
and Praying in your heart of hearts that, 'It Won't Be Too dear.'
You are Simply, at their mercy, When your Boiler is in Dock,
when he Tells you What your Bill will be, 'You nearly, Die With
                                                    Shock.'
Expenses, they go 'Up, and up,' It's impossible, to cope,'
Finally, You 'Just Give Up,' for You have lost, All Hope!'

'Have you tried to get a Plumber?' 'It's enough to make you Sob,'
'When you Need them in a Hurry, 'They are Always, On A Job!'
You Ring around for Other's, as 'Inwardly, You Groan,'
and Finally, When you Do Get Through, 'It's a 'Blinkin,' Answer
                                                    Phone!'
'How Frustrating, Can it Get?' in your 'Desperate, Situation!'
You begin to Wonder, Why it is, 'Life's So Full, of Aggravation.'
If you're lucky enough to get one, where ever  you get one from,
You can 'Bet Your Bottom Dollar,' 'It will Cost a Blooming, Bomb!'

'Oh, 'What a World to live in?' 'It makes me Want to Spew,'
Folk are 'Always, Chasing Money,' 'It is Evil, Through, and
through!'
It sometimes, makes you Wonder, What this Life, is All About?'
if you 'Haven't go the money, 'Then, 'You have to Go, Without.'
As for us 'Poor, Old Pensioner's, 'Life is 'Not all Milk, and Honey,'
it's an 'Up-hill struggle, every day,' and, 'It isn't very Funny,'

Trying to get Jobs done today, is a 'Nightmare, to us all,'
and there's 'Usually a Call Out Charge,' 'How Have They got the
Gall?'
It may be Just a 'Little Job,' but 'That's Where the troubles Start,'
for 'Often, the Cost of Labour,' Is 'More Costly, than the Part!'
When you receive your estimate, Whatever it may be,
What makes it More Expensive, 'Is the Added 'V.A.T.'
If my Mum and Dad, Who are now, Deceased, if Life, was in the
Offin,
When they Saw How much it 'Costs to Live,' They Would 'Jump
Back in their Coffin.'

# DAYS OF GLORY

I can see it all now, as I did when a boy,
heart filled with excitement, and bubbling with joy.
Saturday was Sacred to me in those days,
as I yelled at the top of my voice, 'Up The A's.'
A long line of cars stretched the length of the street,
and all you could see, was Hurrying Feet.

Cup fever spread like a dose of the flu,
as Supporters turned up in their Dark, and Light blue.
A tie drawn at home, always drew a big crowd,
to cheer on their team, of which they were so Proud.
Great was that day, with the atmosphere tense,
as Onlookers tried to climb over the fence.

A chap played the Squeezebox outside of the gate,
whilst Round came the hat, which was held by his mate.
How grateful they were for a Copper, or two,
entertaining us all, as we stood in the queue.
Rosettes of both teams, were proudly displayed,
and souvenir sellers, seemed to do a brisk trade.

Coach upon coach, wound along Greenpond Road,
finding somewhere to park, to deposit their load.
The sunshine broke through from behind a dark cloud,
as the Policeman on horseback, controlled the large crowd.
Click, click, went the turnstile, as the people edged through,
in good time for the Kick Off, at a Quarter past two.
With fingers a tingle, and faces aglow,
came the Loyal Supporters, of 'Old Wathamstow.'

It was Sixpence for adults, and Fourpence for lads,
as excitedly, they clasped the hands of their dad's.
A gaze at the A's, was looked forward by all,
with their Penny for a Programme, and a Penny on the ball.
Before the match started, 'On came the band,'
with Trombones, Trumpets, and Cornets in hand.
They'd play a few marches which sounded a treat,

and then at half time, they'd come round with a sheet.
People threw coins in much to their delight,
as they dropped in their sheet, left, centre, and right.

A loud roar went up, as out the teams came,
at a quarter past two, for the start of the game.
The two Captains met with a shake of the hand,
and the Ref tossed the coin, as I watched from the stand.
The A's won the toss, at their opponents expense,
and the Ref blew the whistle for the game to commence.
After ten minutes play, the Avenue, scored,
I was thrilled with excitement, and How the crowd roared.
Swift, and decisive, the ball seemed to roll,
and everyone said, 'What a cracking good goal.'

Corners were taken, and pennies, changed hands,
as 'Come on you A's could be heard in the stands.
Arguments started, among the huge crowd,
when the other team scored, and their goal disallowed.
The Ref, and the Linesman, began to confide,
with the final decision, that the player was Off side.
'Open yer eyes Ref,' an angry voice spat,
'I reckon he must be as blind as a bat.' ---

When Half time came round, on again, came the band,
and I went for a tea, to the back of the stand.
Up to yet I must say, it had been a good game,
and I hoped that the second half, would be the same.
A nice lump of Tottenham, I had with my tea,
and before the game started, I had a quick pee.
I made my way back to the spot where I stood,
with a glow in my heart, and I felt really good.

As luck would have it, the A's scored again,
the goalkeeper dived, but his dive was in vain.
With a thunderous applause, the crowd, they went mad,
young Jim Lewis had scored with a pass from his dad.
'Hats, Scarves, and Programmes,' were thrown in the air,
and Jubilant faces, was the scene everywhere.

The game got exciting, with Boos from the crowd,
when a Walthamstow Avenue player got fouled.
The Ref's finger pointed to the Penalty spot,
whilst an Avenue player, took his place for the shot.
'Wham went the ball,' as swift as a jet,
as it Crashed with full force, to the back of the net.
Another great cheer for the Avenue team,
and in every aspect, the A's were Supreme.

I will always remember that wonderful game,
and when it had ended, I thought, What a shame.
I shouldered my way with the crowd from the ground,
and excited to think, that we'd reached the Fifth Round.
Folk were discussing the way the team played,
they were proud of the A's, with the skill they displayed.
I heard people say they were glad that they came,
and on everyone's lips, was the Avenue's name.

Tis the end of my story, of those Wonderful days,
no longer will I ever yell, 'Up the A's.'
The days of their glory, lives on in my mind,
from those long years ago, which we've now left behind.
Not once, did I miss any one of their games,
I can still see their faces, and remember their names.
Tears fill my eyes, as my sweet memories flow,
I still cherish the players, of old Walthamstow.
I saw an old Programme, which made me feel sad,
for it brought back the memories, when I was a lad.
I still have the Supporters Club Badge to this day,
and in my treasure chest, that is where it will stay.

I happened to pass by their derelict ground,
as I peeped through the gate, there wasn't a sound.
The sad scene before me, took me by surprise,
I just simply couldn't believe my own eyes.
The Stand was demolished, the Floodlights were down,
with tears in my eyes, my face wore a frown.
For a few sad, brief, moments, my mind wandered back,

when those turnstiles revolved, with a Click and a Clack.
To those thousands of people, who passed through those gates,
holding programmes, and rattles, with their sweethearts, and mates.

Now the team have disbanded, The players, are gone,
along with the memories, that still lingers on.
With an ache in my heart, I continued to stare,
at the Sheer desolation, and Terraces, bare.
As the eerie wind rattled the corrugated fence,
I said to myself, 'This just doesn't make sense.'
I turned on my heel, I could stand it no more,
It was hard to believe, the destruction I saw.
For this Terrible tragedy, 'Who is to blame?
for All that is left, is the Avenue's name. ---

# A TRIBUTE TO DIANA, PRINCESS OF WALES

With the death of Diana, the Whole world still mourns!
She still lives in our hearts with each new day that dawns.
Millions of people simply broke down and cried,
when they learned our beloved Princess Diana had died.
They fell on their knees, and prayed for her Soul!
to Wish her at Peace, after death took its toll.
To this very day, in our hearts, we Still Grieve,
for her Untimely death, is 'So hard to believe!'
Where ever she went, she was 'Belle of the Ball,'
and All over the World, she was loved by us all!
We all share in sorrow, which is Painful to bear,
her beloved two sons, as we kneel down in prayer.

Her Selfless Devotion seemed to stem from her heart,
as she tended the Sick with the love she'd impart.
Sick children would nestle in the crook of her arm,
they adored their Diana, her 'Beauty, her Charm!'
Her words of encouragement, seemed to give them new hope,
To Conquer their illness, when they Could not cope.
For the Good that she did, She seeked No Reward!
and I'm sure now she walks hand in hand with the Lord!
Whatever the ailment, Princess Di showed no fear,
the 'Well-Being of Others, in her heart, she held dear!

Her Great Generosity which she gave, knew no bounds!
and her 'Fund Raising Efforts, realised 'Thousands of Pounds!'
Where ever she was wanted, she answered the Call,
her Shining Example, is a Lesson to us all!'
She will always remain 'A Bright Star in The Sky,'
and remembered with love, till the day that we die!

### 'GOD BLESS YOU DIANA'

## PREVIOUS PUBLICATIONS BY DENNIS J. PENFOLD

### 'POEMS FOR PLEASURE' (VOL 1.2.3.)

### NOSTALGIA STREET'

### 'A BLAST FROM THE PAST'

Dennis Penfold's Biography 'Born To Struggle' is now nearing completion.

It is steeped in memories 'Happy and Sad', containing historical events, and how life was from the 'Twenties to the Forties'.

It is a book to be treasured!

Select Publications